The MP Möller console of the 4/53 organ at St. John's Lutheran Church, Bellevue, Ohio. This console's storied journey began in 1911. Originally built for Möller Opus 1071, Euclid Avenue Presbyterian Church (The Church of the Covenant) Cleveland, Ohio, then sold to Trinity Lutheran Church, Cleveland in 1930. When Trinity replaced the Möller organ in the 1950s, the Toledo Pipe Organ Company acquired it. Ultimately, the Toledo Pipe Organ Company installed the console at St. John's in 1961-62 and the Bunn Minnick Pipe Organ Company of Columbus, Ohio retrofitted and expanded it in 1997-98. (Photo by author)

Making a Joyful Noise:

*History and Evolving Use of the Organs
in a Rural Lutheran Parish
1895-2021*

By

Paul A. Lieber

Partial view of the exposed Great Division, St. John's Lutheran Church. The hooded rank is the 8'
Trompette Heroïque. From middle front to the back 8' Open Diapason, 8' Gemshorn, 16' Violone
(far right), 8' Rohrflute, and the bass of the 8' Open Diapason. (Photo by author)

Library of Congress Control Number: 2023900939

Global ISBN: 978-1-915904-23-2
Hardcover ISBN: 978-1-0880-9895-0

Dedication

*For my family: son Michael, daughter-in-law Jessica,
my grand-daughters Isabella and Evelyn,
and my loving and devoted wife, Karen.*

Contents

Illustrations

Preface

One can easily find organ histories in print that include builders, specifications, and renovations/expansions of many great and famous pipe organs located in cathedrals, large churches, tabernacles, and concert halls. Some notable examples include Severance Hall, Cleveland, Ohio; Woolsey Hall, Yale University, New Haven, Connecticut; Rockefeller Chapel, Chicago, Illinois; both the Mormon Tabernacle and Mormon Convention Center, Salt Lake City, Utah; and The Mother Church, The Church of Christ, Scientist, Boston, Massachusetts, just to name a few. The Organ Historical Society (OHS) Database holds specifications for hundreds of organs with some background for each instrument if available. Having said that, I found it exceptionally rare that a full history of the background and use of individual organs available in print to the public or even their parish. A dearth of information from medium and small churches lucky enough to have pipe organs seemed especially true. In researching some organs in north-central Ohio I found the churches I visited usually had specifications for their instrument, possible builder, and who presently maintained the organ. No further information or historical background was available. This situation appeared to be the norm, not the exception. Thus, I made the decision that my parish, St. John's Lutheran Church, Bellevue, Ohio, would not fall into that category.

When I started researching the organs used at St. John's Lutheran, a parishioner asked me, "It's all well and good that you are writing about the organ, but who is going to read it?" it's a pointed but relevant question. The answer lies in my stylistic choices and strategic approach to writing this historical monograph. First, stylistically I will use both "the author" for a more formal approach where appropriate and as the monograph proceeds to the early 1990s when I was intimately involved in decision-making concerning the organ and I started playing for the Saturday night service in 1995, I will use first person. This stylistic choice reflects the dual audience I want to address. First are organists, musicians, organ historians, and professionals who are conversant with the workings of the pipe organ. The second group comprises St. John's parishioners, local organists and historians, and participants who have played concerts on or with the organ, particularly the former brass and wind ensemble members of Bellevue High School (BHS) Wind Ensemble and Jazz Band.

Second, no matter the stylistic transition from the more formal to the more familiar, the story of the organs of St. John's Lutheran Church, their background, use, and evolution remains central. The organs used at St. John's in many respects paralleled the growth of the parish during the past 125 years. The organs also reflect a story of religious growth and the human story of the parish. The wider use of the organ during the late 1990s and early 2000s represented a quantum leap from the purely religious use of the instrument to a sharing of the organ's capabilities with the community and the surrounding area. Of note was the impact the organ had on teenagers, those Bellevue High School (BHS) athletes who aided in the 1997-98 expansion and renovation of the instrument, four young men who played it for services and concerts, and the BHS musicians who played concerts and some services with it. So, this is not only a history of organs but a human story of a north-central Ohio Lutheran parish, its members, the community, and the youth who embraced it.

Paul A. Lieber, Bellevue, Ohio

Acknowledgements and Sources

I received a great deal of encouragement, support, and assistance from many people and organizations in my quest to write a history of the organs at St. John's Lutheran Church, Bellevue, Ohio. Of special note are J. Clark Wilson, Ellen Middleswarth, and Marlene Buck. First, not only is Clark Wilson a magnificent organist and builder in his own right, but his knowledge of the organ is encyclopedic and his advice, guidance, and support for this project never wavered. Ellen Middleswarth was St. John's Lutheran Church's historian up until her death. Ellen's well-ordered collection of St. John's historical materials was critical to my research, especially during the period 1895-1959. Marlene Buck, who celebrated her 60th year as organist at St. John's (2018), provided several photos during the period 1997-1998 and read/edited parts of the manuscript.

I am indebted to the many people who contributed data, technical support, advice, and editing and proof reading. They are: John Ochenduski, my computer guru who bailed me out of some tight spots and Microsoft Word troubleshooter Rebecca Booze, Mary Lisa Boose, Theodore Buck, Larry Claus, Dr. Erik Knight, Jan LaBonte, Gavin Lepley, Wayne McCoy, Rick Mercier, Dr. Williamson Murray, local Bellevue historian William "Bill" Oddo, Ann Paul, William Van Pelt of the Organ Historical Society, Kristen Rhineberger, Dale Scheid of St. Peter's Lutheran Church, Pontiac, Glenn Taller, Pastors David and Beth Westphal, J. Clark Wilson, Charlotte Zimmerman, and Greg Zimmerman of Zimmerman Construction, and my wife Karen for her patience and indulging my great passion for history and pipe organs.

The organizations that proved to be of immense value to my research were: *The Bellevue Gazette*, The Bellevue Public Library, *The Fremont Weekly Journal*, *The Fremont New-Messenger*, The Fremont Public Library, The Organ Historical Society inclusive of database, The Rutherford B. Hayes Presidential Library, *The Sandusky Register*, St. John's Lutheran Church, and St. Peter's Lutheran Church, Pontiac.

Diamond Jubilee Memory Booklet of the St. John's Evangelical Lutheran Church, Bellevue, Ohio. Published on the Occasion of the Seventy-Fifth Anniversary of the Founding of This Church 1864-1939.

Fremont, Ohio City Directories, 1909 and 1941.

Kinzey, Allen and Sand Lawn, eds. *E.M. Skinner/Aeolian-Skinner Opus List*, New Revised Edition. Richmond, Virginia: The Organ Historical Society, 1997.

Kuntz, Reverend John Waldemar. *Short History of St. John's Lutheran Church Bellevue, Ohio, Huron County*. Bellevue, OH: Press of the Gazette Publishing Company, 1914.

Petty, Bynum. *An Organ A Day. The Enterprising Spirit of M.P. Möller*. Hillsdale, NY: Pendragon Press, 2013.

St. John's Lutheran Church Council Minutes, 1895-2000, Bellevue, Ohio.

St. John's Lutheran Church Service Bulletins, Recital and Concert Programs.

St. *Peter's Lutheran Church Council Minutes, Pontiac, Ohio.*

Foreword

The present exhaustive work by Paul Lieber represents one of the most in-depth histories of a church's pipe organ that I have ever seen – truly unusual for anything less than one of the Great Churches of the world. His narrative is chock-full of interesting information on the parish's buildings, instruments, musicians, organ builders, the congregation, and local personalities and citizenry. He chronicles the organs' saga to hold the casual reader's attention, as well as offering much detail aimed at the well-initiated.

Anyone with an interest in the King of Instruments in general or in the musical history of St. John's will find a wealth of information and a resource well worth the read!

Clark Wilson

September 2021

Introduction

"And all the people went up following him, playing pipes, and rejoicing greatly, so that the Earth quaked at their noise."

I Kings 1:40

The year 2014 was of great significance to the congregation of St. John's Lutheran Church, Bellevue, Ohio, for on June 10, 1864, the church was founded. It seemed only proper that during our sesquicentennial year a history of the organs of St. John's be initiated. Starting in 1895 St. John's has been blessed with four pipe organs: An organ from a local builder John H. Sole of Fremont, Ohio; the Knapp Memorial Organ, its origin and manufacturer at this point are unknown (1933); an organ from the Toledo Pipe Organ Company for the "new" church (1962), a major renovation and expansion of that organ by the Bunn Minnick Pipe Organ Company of Columbus, Ohio (1997-98), the addition of an EM Skinner 8' English Horn in 2003, and essential rank replacement and major tonal redesign of the organ by Clark Wilson and Glenn Tallar during 2018-2021. Over the church's 150-year history, the primary use of these instruments has been, and remains, leading worship services. But with the expansion and renovation of the organ in 1997-98, the church's use of the organ evolved as the congregation shared its newly rebuilt and expanded organ with the community at large holding three concerts with the Bellevue High School Wind Ensemble, two young organist concerts, and Clark Wilson's performance of orchestral transcriptions and accompaniment four silent films from the 1920s on the organ.

This history of the organs of St. John's Lutheran Church covers the specifics of each organ if known, dates when used, and the concert programs played on each of the instruments. Having researched the organs of St. John's, this church, and for that matter any church, needs more than good instruments for the musical leadership of the church to be a success. The church needs dedicated and talented individuals to not only play the organs, but individuals who are willing to put the immense time required to choose the appropriate music, practice preludes, offertories, postludes, choir accompaniment, different liturgical settings, weddings, funerals, and several hundred hymns of both a traditional and a contemporary bent. Over the years St. John's has indeed been fortunate to have organists who met that challenge: Adolph Frenz, Henry Ebertshaeuser, Magdalena Sutter Knapp, Anna Sutter, Katherine Lehmann, Helen Mohr Ahn, Helen Hildebrand Bauer, Jessie Kistler Ebert, Iona Miller Eleazer, Grace Morris, Marlene Buck, our longest serving organist (1958-2020), Paul Lieber (1995-present) for the Saturday evening worship service, and Christopher Meadows.

It should be noted that Marlene Buck was the only organist to play *all* the pipe organs used at St. John's Lutheran Church. She played the Sole organ at St. Peter's Lutheran Church for services as a teenager, the Knapp Memorial Organ as assistant organist, and all others as the assistant organist or senior organist at St. John's.

The Sole Organ (1895-1933)

Born in London, England on December 5, 1860, John H. Sole went on to apprentice with W.H. Hill & Sons church organ builders at age 15. During his apprenticeship with Hill, Sole helped in the building of several large instruments: Westminster Abbey, St. Paul's Cathedral, York Minster, Worcester Cathedral, and the Town Hall Organ of Adelaide, Australia. In 1881, Mr. Sole emigrated to The United States and took up work with the Roosevelt Organ Company in New York City. He moved to Boston in 1883 taking a position with the Hook & Hastings Company until 1886. Sole worked with the George S. Hutchings Organ Company until 1888, when he left that firm and started his own organ business. In May 1894, Sole moved westward and settled permanently in Fremont, Ohio, where he established his own well-equipped organ building company.

On January 17, 1896, The Fremont Weekly Journal ran an article that read:

"The latest product of this factory is a large two manual organ built for St. John's Lutheran Church, Bellevue, Ohio. Several new organs are now in course of construction, notably among them being a large $3,000 organ for St. John's German Lutheran Church of Richmond, Indiana. Mr. Sole is favorably known as an honorable and enterprising businessman, while his productions give eminent satisfaction."

The Bellevue Lutheran Parish was fortunate to have an organization known as the Organ Club later renamed the Cotta Society. The Organ Club's chief objective was to raise the needed funds for the purchase and installation of an organ. The cost to the parish was $1500. St. John's took possession of a tracker action organ built by John Sole of Fremont, Ohio in 1895. A dedication service was held for the new red brick church and organ on July 21, 1895. As stated in the *Short History of St. John's Evangelical Lutheran Church* by The Reverend John Waldemar Kuntz, The Organ Club's objective "was accomplished and the present pipe organ is a fitting monument to its memory."

In the early 1930s the Sole organ was removed from St. John's except for the bottom 18 pipes of the 8' Open Diapason. These 18 diapason pipes were kept as a facade in preparation for the installation of an organ purchased by Frank A. Knapp in memory of his daughter, Stella Knapp-Sykes. St. John's donated the Sole organ minus the façade pipes to St. Peter's Lutheran Church, Pontiac (Monroeville, Ohio, mailing address) where it remains today in an unaltered condition, except for the 18 Diapason pipes. The original Sole wood winding is still in use and can be seen on entry into the pipe chamber at St. Peter's.

The tracker action organ built by John Sole of Fremont, Ohio as seen in the sanctuary of St. John's Lutheran Church, Bellevue, Ohio in an undated photograph. More than likely the photo was taken in the early 1900s (St. John's Lutheran Church photo archives).

The following specifications and details of the unaltered John H. Sole tracker action organ were compiled on May 23, 2014, at St. Peter's Lutheran Church of Pontiac, by the author with the aid of Mr. Larry Claus. Larry Claus, with the help of John Cox, Dale Scheid, Sharon Scheid and others, had restored the organ to working condition.

Pipe Organ Specification: 2 manuals, 10 ranks, 558 total pipes, with one rank extending to 16'

Great

8' Open Diapason	spotted metal, sc. 58 @ tenor C, ca*
8' Dulciana	spotted metal, sc 68 @ tenor C
8' Melodia	wood, sc. 1 ½" x 1 ¾" @ mid C
4' Octave	spotted metal, sc. 73 @ tenor C
2' Super Octave	spotted metal, sc. 84 @ tenor C

Swell to Great (there are two of these; only one is in working condition)
Swell to Pedal (not a mistake; on Great side)

Swell

8' Salicional	spotted metal, sc. 58 @ tenor C
8' Stopped Diapason Treble	stopped wood for Treble, sc. 1 15/16" x 1 1/8" @ mid C
8' Stopped Diapason Bass	
8' Oboe	common metal, sc. 3 5/16" @ low C
8' Bassoon	

| 4' Flute Harmonique | spotted metal, sc. 70 @ tenor C |
| Swell Tremolo | |

Pedal

| 16' Ped. Bourdon | stopped wood, sc. 5 1/8 "x 4 1/16" @ tenor C |
| Great to Pedal | |

*The bottom 18 pipes of the 8' Open Diapason were kept at St. John's Bellevue for use as façade pipes for the Knapp Memorial Organ.

Console Details:

| Manual Compass- | 61 notes |
| Pedal Compass- | 27 notes (flat pedal board) |

Indicator Light for the blower; Wind gauge on console not hooked up; Bellows Signal no longer working Entire organ under expression; Swell Shoe; Forte Pedal brings Great into play; Piano Pedal brings into play 8' Dulciana and 8' Melodia; Plate on Console: "John H. Sole Fremont, Ohio" Forte and Piano Plates not on console and in possession of Mr. Larry Claus.

Blower is of unknown origin having no distinguishing marks or name plates.

Photo of the Sole organ Great Division. From left to right the 8' Open Diapason, 8' Dulciana, 8' Melodia, 4' Octave, and 2' Super Octave. The photo below is of the Pedal 16' Bourdon. The organ is located at St. Peter's Lutheran Church, Pontiac, just outside of Monroeville, Ohio and is used every Sunday. See page 93 for additional photos of this instrument. (Photos by the author)

On Sunday, July 22, 1900, St. John's Lutheran Church celebrated its five-year anniversary in its newly built red brick church. The morning service was in German and the evening service was in English. The next evening, there was an organ recital and sacred concert bringing the anniversary celebration to a close. The builder of our organ, Mr. John H. Sole, sang a baritone solo for the concert. The program and performers were as follows:

1. Chant des Voyaguers	*Paderewski*	
Marcia Villereccia	*Fumagalli*	Prof. A.D. Scammell
2. The Penitent	*B. Van de Water*	Miss Lula B. Bowman
3. Hymne a Sainte Cecile	*Gounod*	Mr. F. Wickert
4. Baritone Solo	*Selected*	Mr. John H. Sole
5. Solo	*Selected*	Miss Bowman
6. Grand Offertoires in F	*Batiste*	Miss Anna Sutter
7. The Heavenly Song	Gray	Miss Clara Biebrichter
8. Fugue in E Minor	*J.S. Bach*	Mr. Wickert
9. Immortality	*Edna Rosalind Park*	
O, Rest in the Lord	*Mendelsohn*	Miss Stella M. Latham
10. Improvisation, showing resources of the organ		Prof. A.D. Scammell

Fourteen years later, during the pastorate of The Reverend John W. Kuntz, the author's great-grandfather, St. John's Lutheran celebrated its 50th anniversary of the parish's founding (1864-1914). During the week of June 14-17, 1914, various activities commemorating the church's 1864 founding took place. Among these were a sacred music concert held on Tuesday evening, June 16. Quoting from the concert program, "Organist and choir will render the following Sacred Concert."

Miss Eva E. Lehman of Canton, Ohio, Soprano

Overture Euryanthe	Weber
Unfold Ye Portals	Gounod
Senior Choir	
Soprano Solo	
Spring Song	Macfarlane
The Little Brown Church	Pitt-Hall
Male Quartet	
Duet "In Peace with Thee"	G.B. Nevin
Miss Eva Lehman and W.H. Lehman	
I'm a Pilgrim	I.B. Wilson
St. John's Choir	
Idyll	Kinder
Chansonette	Van Blon
Galilee	Kirkpatrick
Male Quartet	
Soprano Solo	
Zion Awake	Costa
St. John's Choir	
Postlude	Tousa

Katherine Lehman, Organist

The Sole organ provided regular and faithful service to the congregation of St. John's Lutheran until the late fall of 1933, when problems apparently started to arise. According to the council minutes, a special meeting of the church council was held on November 19, 1933.

"A special meeting of the church council was held in the church after service this morning. Rev. Ahn reported T.V. Conner Sons called to tune the organ and reported certain repairs would have to be made. He called on Mr. Knapp and Mr. Knapp agreed to install a modern Mohler (sic) Electric organ and remove the present organ as a memorial gift in memory of his departed daughter Stella. This gift which will enhance our services is highly appreciated by all members and shows Mr. Knapp's interest in the welfare of our church. On motion of H. Erf seconded by Carl Zehner the offer was accepted by a rising vote of thanks."

The disposition of the Sole organ can be traced in the winter and spring 1934 monthly council meeting minutes of both St. John's Bellevue and St. Peter's Lutheran Church, Pontiac. At the January 31, 1934, meeting of St. John's council: "C.W. Schug made a motion trustees to be authorized to sell the old pipe organ for whatever they could get, second by Wm. Hankammer (sic), carried."

The February 26, 1934, St. John's council meeting ended any doubt about the final disposition of the Sole organ. "I.R. Felker reported Prof Sole of Fremont inspected the old organ for Pontiac congregation and asked for the tuning pipes. Inasmuch as these are ready to be sold and the old organ will soon be worthless stored in the cellar. Carl Zehner moved we give the old organ to Pontiac and after it is set up they may pay us what they feel it is worth to them seconded by S. Trigg carried."

St. Peter's Lutheran Church, Pontiac, held a congregational meeting on May 13, 1934, and voted to have the organ dedication recital on May 20, 1934. The Sole organ has served the congregation at St. Peter's from 1934 to the present day. With the exception of the façade pipes, the organ is extant and playable. This organ is one of the very few Sole organs in existence unaltered, let alone playable.

John Sole's organ building business did not fare quite as well as the organ he built for St. John's. In the Thursday, October 3, 1901, Fremont Journal, the newspaper ran an article about the disastrous fire that destroyed John Sole's organ manufacturing concern:

"The building on Hickory Street (sic) formerly occupied by Beery & Davis but which was leased by John H. Sole when vacated by the former firm was entirely destroyed by fire Saturday. For several years Mr. Sole has been manufacturing pipe organs in the building and had several organs nearly completed.

The fire started in the engine room and the flames spread very rapidly. Mr. Sole and Adam Bletscher who were at work in the machine shop adjoining noticed the fire almost as soon as it started but were unable to save anything except Bletscher's tools.

An alarm was at once turned in, but the fire department did not respond promptly to the call and when it did arrive at the fire it was discovered that there were no water mains on the street, the nearest hydrant being at the corner of Napoleon and Jefferson streets (sic), and they did not have enough hose to lay a line from that. Finally after going back to the engine house and securing more hose one stream of water was turned on the fire, but the pressure was so poor little could be done and the entire building and contents were totally destroyed.

The house of Henry Miller was also so badly burned as to be worthless.

Mr. Sole's loss will be about $10,000 with no insurance as he allowed his policies to lapse a short time ago. The loss of Beery & Davis is partially covered by insurance.

Although he lost heavily by the fire Mr. Sole was not disheartened and at once made arrangements to secure other quarters and on Tuesday closed negotiations for the lease of the two-story brick building, corner of Justice and Front streets (sic), known as the Gusdorf property and started to work on Wednesday. He has the kind of nerve and pluck that is bound to succeed and he will soon have a larger establishment than before."

Not much in historical material remains on John Sole and his organ manufacturing. He is listed in the Fremont, Ohio, City Directory, 1909, as "builder of Church and Chapel organs, h 1421 Napoleon: B. phone 58" and in the 1941 Fremont City Directory under businesses as "Organ Manufacturers, Sole Jno H 1421 Napoleon."

According to a short article in The Fremont News-Messenger dated December 15, 1945, John Sole passed away in his home. On December 17, 1945, The Fremont News-Messenger ran an obituary on Sole providing a brief history, naming survivors, and stating that funeral services would be held in his home at 2:30 pm on Tuesday.

The Knapp Memorial Organ (1934-1959)

It has been difficult, to say the least, to find detailed information on the so-called Knapp Memorial Organ or as noted in the council minutes, "a modern Mohler Electric organ." In the first place, the term "Mohler" probably means the MP Möller Organ Company of Hagerstown, Maryland. Möller was the most prolific pipe organ builder in U.S. history, making over 11,800 organs from 1875-1992. Utilizing the services of Mr. William Van Pelt of the Organ Historical Society (OHS) in the search of the Knapp Memorial Organ's Opus number, Van Pelt found no organ listed for St. John's Lutheran Church or any other church in Bellevue, Ohio, built by the Möller Organ Company in the entire history of the firm. It is possible that Mr. Frank Knapp bought a Möller organ that had been in use at another church or site. I do know the organ had two manuals and 12 stops.

Not only did St. John's receive a "new" organ during this time, but the congregation was shocked to find itself involved in a messy domestic dispute between Reverend A.A. Ahn and his wife, Helen Mohr Ahn, the church organist. The following are excerpts from the church special council meetings dealing with this situation.

"Bellevue, O January 12, 1934. A special meeting of the church council was held at Schug's Hardware Store 7:30 pm this evening…moved by L. Linder seconded by Chas. Dehe that committee be elected to ask Rev. Ahn not to fill the pulpit and Mrs. Ahn not to play the organ until further action by church council carried."

Undated photo of the interior of the 1895 church edifice. The façade pipes of the "Mohler" organ can plainly be seen. The two manual console is barely visible at the far left in front of the choir members.

On the very day the "new Mohler" organ was first used; another special meeting of the church council took place.

"January 14, 1934, a special meeting of the parish council was held after the service this morning. Court action brought by Mrs. Ahn this past week for separate maintenance from Rev. Ahn…made it necessary for him to submit his resignation as our pastor.
His resignation in writing was given to the Sec'y and read at this meeting.
On a motion from by I.R. Felker, second by L. Linder this was accepted."

On Sunday, January 14, 1934, the "new Mohler" organ was first used by the church for a service. The Monday, January 15, 1934, The Bellevue Gazette ran a short article titled, *Memorial Organ Heard First Time in Lutheran Church*:

"Music from the recently installed memorial organ was heard for the first time Sunday during morning and evening services in St. John's Lutheran Church, Miss Helen Hildebrand was organist."
"Installation of the organ, a recent gift to the church from Frank A. Knapp, has just been completed. A formal dedication and recital is planned at a later date. At Sunday morning services in St. John's recently elected church officers were installed, and at the evening services Rev. A.K. Boerger of Hamilton, presented a lecture on Persia."

The formal dedication of the Knapp Memorial Organ took place at the Sunday morning service on January 28, 1934. The Saturday, January 27, 1934, edition of The Bellevue Gazette ran both the morning dedication service and the organ recital program. "Presentation of the memorial organ by Mrs. Wm. C. Henry on behalf of donors, Mr. and Mrs. Frank A. Knapp. Acceptance of the memorials, Mr. I.R. Felker on behalf of the congregation." The dedication recital was held on Sunday afternoon.

> Chimes---Miss Helen Hildebrand, organist
> Scripture Reading---Dr. Emmanuel Poppen
> Fantasia and Fugue---S. Archer Gibson
> Willow Whisper from "Across the Infinite" ---R. Dean Shure
> Neptune---from Sea Sketches" ---R.S. Stoughton
> Nocturne---G. Ferrata
>   Mr. Frederick C. Mayer
> Violin Solo---Adoration---Thos. Aigler
> Vocal Solo "How Beautiful the Mountains" Edna Endle Brown
> Offertory---Andante in G---Batiste---Miss Helen Hildebrand
> Fantasia on "Bells of Abardovey" ---H.J. Stewart
> Marche Champetre---A.G. Boex
> "Ein feste Burg" ---Carl Stein
>   Mr. Frederick C. Mayer
> Benediction

The regular monthly council meeting convened on January 31, 1934. "Mrs. Ahn presented her resignation in writing as organist which was accepted on motion by Carl Zehner seconded by Chas. Dehe," according to the meeting minutes. At this same meeting, the council elected Helen Hilderbrand to fill the remainder of Mrs. Ahn's term as organist.

On December 15, 1935, a dedication service was held in which the Knapp Memorial Organ played a prominent role. Frank Knapp donated new chancel furniture designed and made especially for St. John's Lutheran by the Liturgical Guild of Cleveland, Ohio in memory of his departed wife, Magdalena Sutter Knapp (1861-1933). The hand carved altar and associated furniture is still in use today in the present (1962) church. The December 15, 1935, dedication service is presented here in full.

Prelude—Violin Solo---"Die Meistersinger," by Richard Wagner   Thomas Aigler
              Organ Accompaniment, Mrs. F.T. Ebert
Processional Hymn 140---"Holy, Holy, Holy"
The Order of the Morning Service (Page 7)
Confession and Absolution (Page 8)
The Introit and Gloria Patri
The Kyrie, Gloria in Excelsis and the Collect
The Nicene Creed (Page 14)
Anthem---"Sing Unto the Lord," Wilson   Choir
Presentation of Knapp Memorial   Mrs. Wm. C. Henry
              Dedication---Rev. Paul A. Rempe
Hymn 79---"I Love Thy Zion, Lord"
Sermon   Rev. W.E. Schuette, D.D.
          (Pastor of St. John's, 1893-1901)
Vocal Solo---"How Lovely Are Thy Dwellings,"   Samuel Liddle
             Edna Endle-Brown
Offertory Hymn 87---"My Church, My Church, My Dear Old Church"
The Prayer and The Lord's Prayer
Benediction and Doxology
Recessional Hymn 158---"Love Divine, All Love Excelling"
Postlude---"Ecclesia Marcia," by M. McCabe Day
             Mrs. F.T. Ebert

The period 1934-1945 saw its share of dedication and anniversary celebrations at St. John's. On October 1, 1939, at, The Diamond Jubilee Services (1864-1939) made for another opportunity for the Knapp Organ to lead an important anniversary service.

Silent Prayer
Piano-Organ Prelude: "Adoration"   Felix Borowski
         Iona Miller, organ and Arlene Middleswarth, piano
Processional Hymn: "Holy, Holy, Holy"
Invocation, Confession, and Absolution
The Introit and Gloria Patri, Kyrie
The Gloria in Excelsis and the Collect
The Epistle: Ephesians 4: 4-16

The Gradual and the Hallelujah
The Gospel: Matthew 16: 13-18
The Apostles' creed
Anthem (Junior Choir): "Sent Out Thy Light"   Gounod
Hymn: "Glorious Things of Thee Are Spoken"
Anniversary Sermon: The Reverend W.E. Schuette, D.D. Sewickley, PA.,
          President of the Eastern District of the American Lutheran Church
Anthem (Senior Choir): "Thank God for Blessings"   Warrick-Ward Stephens
Offertory Hymn: "I Love Thy Zion Lord"
The Prayer and the Lord's Prayer
The Benediction and Doxology
Recessional Hymn: "The Church Is One Foundation"
Silent Prayer
Organ Postlude: "Festival Postludium"   John Herman Loud
          Iona Miller

The Knapp Organ played a significant role in St. John's celebration of 50 years in the church edifice on Sunday morning, November 18, 1945. What follows are the musical components of the service:

Organ-Piano Prelude:
          "Sheep May Safely Graze" (from Birthday Cantata) J.S. Bach
                    Mrs. Roland Morris, Miss Ellen Smetzer
Processional Hymn: "Holy, Holy, Holy"
Vocal Solo: "The Lord Is My Light" (Psalm 27)   Frances Allitsen
                    Mrs. Ruth Paul
Hymn: "Glorious Things of Thee are Spoken"
Anthem (Senior Choir): "Praise Ye the Lord"   Molitor-Goldsworthy
Offertory Hymn: "My Church, My Church"
Recessional Hymn: "The Church's One Foundation"
Organ Postlude, Mrs. Roland Morris

The Knapp Memorial Organ was in use from 1934-1959 until the demolition of the 1895 red brick edifice to make room for a new church to be built on the same site. The congregation broke ground on the "new" (present-day) church on August 14, 1960, the cornerstone being laid on October 23, 1960. During 1953-1954 St. John's had built a new Parish Hall. It was in the upstairs of this building in the Fellowship Hall that church services were held until the new sanctuary building was completed in January 1962.

The Toledo Pipe Organ Company Organ and Transition (1955-1996)

Located in the Great division of the Toledo Pipe Organ Company organ, the 4' Flute Harmonique pictured as it is now, in the Swell Division of the present instrument. (Photo by author)

At its November 23, 1955, meeting, the church council contracted a new company to maintain the organ. "It was moved by Harland Erf and seconded by O.C. Schaaf and carried that $180 per year be paid to the Toledo Pipe Organ Company for maintenance of the church pipe organ per contract."

With the building of a new church the subject of whether to keep the Knapp Memorial Organ, expand it, or replace it with a larger instrument came to the fore. The program for the first organ recital held on Sunday, May 20, 1962, briefly outlined the decision that the committee reached.

"The four manual Moller organ of 34 sets and 2614 pipes, was a gift of Mrs. Allan Aigler, Mrs. Herbert Erf, Mrs. Herman Thornton, and Dr. Sara Sykes Magnuson. It was installed by the Toledo Pipe Organ Company under the direction of Mr. Julian Bulley.

"In planning for the new church, the committee gave serious study to enlarging the twelve stop Moller organ given in 1933 by Mr. and Mrs. Knapp, but when the opportunity came to purchase the larger organ as a unit, the diverse tonal resources appeared to be a great asset."

The Toledo Pipe Organ Company (TPOC) instrument was donated in the memory of Mr. and Mrs. Frank A. Knapp, Mrs. Stella Knapp Sykes, and Mrs. Alice Knapp Henry. The total cost of the organ and the installation was $15,600 plus the TPOC took possession of the Knapp Memorial Organ of 1933.

According to Julian Bulley, the TOPC (Möller) organ installed at St. John's came from Central Methodist Church in Lansing, Michigan. Some pipes were taken from a Möller organ located in Cleveland, Ohio (*letter to Paul Lieber from Julian Bulley dated October 22, 1993*).

I pursued Bulley's off-hand comment that some pipes from a Cleveland church were included in the organ from the Toledo Pipe Organ Company. With the aid of Clark Wilson and the Organ Historical Society Pipe Organ Database, I found that St. John's was the third church to make use of the Solo 8' Stentorphone. Not only was the 8' Stentorphone used in two churches prior to St. John's, but so was the oak four manual Möller console. On the underside of the console lid, "Church of the Covenant, Cleveland" was written in blue-green grease pencil. Both the console and the 8' Stentorphone were originally from the M.P. Möller Opus 1071 built and installed in the Euclid Avenue Presbyterian Church, now known as The Church of the Covenant, in 1911. Opus 1071 was composed of five divisions, 35 stops, 48 registers, and 37 ranks. The organ was replaced in 1930 by E.M Skinner Opus 844 and sold to Trinity Lutheran Church of Cleveland,

Ohio. The Möller organ remained at Trinity Lutheran until it was replaced by a von Beckerath instrument. Subsequently Opus 1071 was sold to the TPOC, and they used the console and the 8' Stentorphone for St. John's Lutheran, Bellevue (*OHS Pipe Organ Database*).

I will use the much more complete inventory of the organ that The Bunn Minnick Pipe Organ Company produced as part of its 1995 proposal to repair and expand the Toledo Pipe Organ Company instrument. *It should be noted that the divisions in the organ were listed by Bunn Minnick as Great, Choir, Swell, Solo, and Pedal in that order, reason unknown. This is NOT the author's divisional order. This divisional order reflects the order in which all documents supplied to St. John's Lutheran Church by Bunn Minnick.*

The Toledo Pipe Organ Company Specification: 4 Manuals, 36 ranks, 2,353 Total Pipes, with 6 Ranks extending to 16'

Great:

16' Quintadena   Rank 1   73 capped metal pipes
(1st note main chest ten F:1173 HJ Clark 12/10 – 1st spotted sc 66; mid C sc 72/71)

8' Open Diapason   Rank 2   61 metal pipes
(stamped sc 40; mid C up common metal)

8' Gemshorn   Rank 3   61 wood and metal pipes
(1-12 tapered wood; 13-61 common metal; tc, sc 58 @mouth)

8' Quintadena   from rank #1

8' Melodia   Rank 4   61 wood pipes
(1-12 stopped, CC 3 ½"x3"; tc 2 ½"x 2 1/16")

4' Octave   Rank 5   73 metal pipes
(bass zinc; ten F common metal; sc tc 70; inscribed L Holmes OCT)

4' Flute Harmonique   Rank 6   61 metal pipes
(bass zinc; tc sc 68; Mid C sc 75 Harm7/32" hole)

2' Super Octave   from rank #5

III Mixture   Rank 7-9   183 metal pipes
("new" 2 2/3' sc 68; 2' sc 72; 1 1/3' sc 79; Breaks 36/37, 48/49, stamped Holland)

8' Tromba   from rank #33

4' Great to Great (originally was a 4' Clarion until replaced by Julian Bulley in February 1994)

(Great: 9 ranks, 573 pipes)

Choir:

8' Geigen Diapason   Rank 10   73 pipes
(Ten F stamped 3005 GIRN F; sc 68 @ ten F, lead; mid C sc 68)

8' Gamba   from rank #36

8' Concert Flute   Rank 11   73 pipes
(mid C sc 2 ⅛"x2 ⅜"; #37 wood harmonic sc 1 ½" x1 ¾")

8' Dulciana   Rank 12   73 pipes
(tc sc 70)

8' Unda Maris (tc)	Rank 13	49 pipes
(tc stamped 3005 UMR C; inscribed CR; sc 72)		
4' Flute D' Amour	Rank 14	73 pipes
(stopped wood; CC scale 3 3/16"x3 1/8"; tc sc 1 7/8"x2 1/4")		
2' Harmonic Piccolo		from rank 14
(duplex action)		
8' Clarinet	Rank 15	61 pipes
(typical Möller; adjustable caps; sc 1 ¾" inscribed WP 6" Reg. A 440 JR)		
Tremolo		
(Blank Knob)		

(Choir: 6 ranks, 402 pipes)

Swell:

16' Bourdon	Rank 16	73 pipes
(mid C sc 2 7/8"x3 ½"; ink stamped 1171)		
8' Open Diapason	Rank 17	73 pipes
(stamped OCT)		
8' Gedeckt	Rank 18	73 pipes
(tc sc 3 5/16"x2 5/8"; mid C 2 ¼"x1 7/8")		
8' Flute Traverso	Rank 19	73 pipes
(1-12 stopped wood; 13-73 open wood; tc 3 1/16"x2 3/4"; mid C 2 3/16"x1 7/8")		
8' Viole	Rank 20	73 pipes
(stamped V.D. Orch 64 C; sc 77)		
8' Voix Celeste (tc)	Rank 21	61 pipes
(mid C sc 74)		
8' Aeoline	Rank 22	73 pipes
4' Principal	Rank 23	73 pipes
4' Flute		from rank #18
2' Flautino	Rank 24	61 pipes
(sc 74)		
III Dolce Cornet	Rank 25-26	121 pipes (should be 122)
(2 2/3' spotted; sc 70; 1 3/5' spotted sc 79 top octave breaks back; knob draws 2' from rank #24)		
8' Trompette	Rank 27	61 pipes
(not a Trompette but a Cornopean; tc sc 3 ¾", #37 first harmonic; stamped 5 ½ HAR C. C)		
8' Oboe	Rank 28	61 pipes
(tc sc 2 1/2")		
8' Vox Humana	Rank 29	61 pipes
(sc 1 3/4")		
Tremolo		

(Swell: 14 ranks, 937 pipes)

Solo:

8' Open Diapason	Rank 30	61 pipes
(marked Stentorphone; CC scale 38)		
8' Major Flute	Rank 31	61 pipes
(open wood gross flute; sc 5 5/8"x4 3/4")		
8' Gross Gamba	Rank 32	61 pipes
(inscribed 1164 C Viol D Orch F.T. Clark)		
16' Trombone	Rank 33	85 pipes
8' Tromba		from rank # 33
4' Clarion		from rank # 33
Tremolo		
Chimes		
(Blank Knob)		

(Solo: 4 ranks, 268 pipes)

Pedal:

16' Double Open Diapason	Rank 34	32 pipes; wood
(sc 17x14; not original; reportedly Casavant)		
16' Bourdon	Rank 35	56 pipes; wood
(typical Möller large scale)		
16' Violone	Rank 36	85 pipes
(1-12 full length open wood; 13-24 zinc; 25-85 spotted metal; #25 marked 3005; Gamba C; sc 70)		
16' Lieblich Gedeckt		from rank #16
16' Quintadena		from rank #1
8' Bass Flute		from rank #35
8' Violin Cello		from rank #36
4' Flute		from rank #35
16' Trombone		from rank #33
8' Tromba		from rank #33
4' Clarion		from rank # 33

(Pedal: 3 ranks, 173 pipes)

Couplers: (located on name board)

Great, Swell, Choir, Solo to Pedal; 4 Great, 4 Swell, 4 Choir, 4 Solo to Pedal.

Swell, Choir, Solo to Great; 16 Swell to Great, 16 Choir to Great, 16 Solo to Great.

4 Swell to Great, 4 Choir to Great, 4 Solo to Great.

Choir to Swell, 4' Choir to Swell, 16 Swell, 4 Swell.

Swell, Solo to Choir, 16 Swell to Choir, 16 Solo to Choir; 4 Swell to Choir,

4 Solo to Choir; 16 Choir, 4 Choir.

16 Solo, 4 Solo.

Miscellaneous Console Controls:

Great, Swell, Choir, and Solo Unison Release (on/off push button all located on key cheek)

Schulmerich Bells Control Panel

Voltmeter

1-6+0	Full Organ Pistons (located under left side of Solo manual)
1-6+0	Solo Pistons (located under the center of the Solo manual)
1-6+0	Pedal Pistons (located under left side of Swell manual)
1-6+0	Swell Pistons (located under center of Swell manual)
1-6+0	Great Pistons (located under center of Great manual)
1-6+0	Choir Pistons (located under center of Choir manual)

Sforzando Reversible Toe Stud; Great, Swell, Choir to Pedal Reversible Toe Stud.

Swell Expression Pedal; Great/Choir/Solo Expression Pedal; Crescendo Pedal, 5 Crescendo Indicator Lights; Sforzando Indicator Light

The blower is Kinetic: 5" @ 2200 cfm; 10" @250 cfm; 1150 rpm, 3 phase, 220 volt, 5 hsp.

"The organ is reported to be based on Opus 3005; however, the following Opus numbers appear on the pipes:"

3005: Great: 8 Diapason, 4 Octave; Choir: 8 Gemshorn, 8 Unda Maris, 8 Gamba, 8 Geigen
       Principal; Swell: 8 Viole, 8 Celeste, 4 Octave, 2 Flautino, III Cornet (Möller)

1071: Solo: 8 Stentorphone (Möller, Church of the Covenant, Presbyterian, 1911) 4/79

2376: Solo: 8 Stentorphone (both numbers appear) Scottish Rite Cath-Williamsport, PA 3/40

1173: Great: 16 Quintadena-Masonic Temple-Youngstown, OH 2/41

2617: Great: 4 Flute Harmonique Carron Street Baptist-PGH 2/19

 936: Choir: 8 Dulciana St. Paul's P.E.-Detroit-, MI 3/48

1164: Solo: 8 VDO Moravian-Bethlehem, PA 3/55

8767: Solo: 16 Trombone (Dennison rank)

2604: Swell: 8 Diapason (Stamped Octave) McPhail Music School-Minneapolis, MN 2/13

1153: Swell: 8 Aeoline Shinkle Methodist-Covington, KY 2/20

1171: Swell: 8 Bourdon Coke College (1910) Hartsville, SC 2/19

New Organ At Lutheran Church

"Mrs. Roland (Grace) Morris, organist of St. John's Lutheran Church, shown at the console of the "new" four manual organ installed in the new church building. At present only two manuals are in use. When the organ has been completely installed, an organ recital is planned." Photo and quotes from The Bellevue Gazette, January 18, 1962.

Dedication of the new church sanctuary took place on Sunday, January 14, 1962, at 3:00 p.m. The new church edifice cost $380,000 (in 2021 dollars $3,409,588.39) and had a seating capacity of 675 people, but according to the January 15th (Monday) issue of *The Bellevue Gazette*, more than 1,000 people attended the dedication service. Mrs. Roland (Grace) Morris, St. John's senior organist, played the service on the "new" four manual, 36 rank TPOC organ.

Prelude:
    "Es ist das Heil"   Unknown
    "Allein Gott"   Walther
    "Lobe den Herren" (chorales)   Walther
Processional Hymn:
    "Lobe den Herren" (Praise to the Lord)   Gesangbuch
Senior Choir Anthem: "Open the Gates of the Temple"   Knapp
Hymn: "Glorious Things of Thee Are Spoken"   Austrian Hymn
Offertory: "Toccata per l'Elvantione"   Frescobaldi
Junior Choir Anthem: "Hallelujah"   Lewandowski
Combined Choir Anthem: "Faith of Our Fathers"   St. Catherine
Recessional Hymn: "Now Thank We All Our God"   "Gratitude"
Postlude: "Ein Feste Burg"   Pachelbel

On Saturday, January 20, 1962, the first wedding ceremony, Carol Sue Andrews to Gary R. Weller, took place in the new sanctuary. The Tuesday 'Society News" of *The Bellevue Gazette* carried the story:

"Mrs. Theodore Buck, a friend and assistant organist, was at the console of the organ for a program of music preceding the ceremony. Selections included "I Love Thee," "Salut d' Amour," "Suite Gothique," "On Wings of Song," "Calm as the Night," "Evening Star," and "Traumereu." She also played softly during the ceremony.

Roger Russell, a friend, was soloist. Preceding the ceremony, he sang "O Lord Most Holy," "O Perfect Love," "Wedding Prayer," and while the couple knelt, "The Lord's Prayer."

The newness of the church and the music gave an air of elegance to the open church service which was attended by nearly 400 relatives and friends of the young couple."

The first organ recital on the TPOC organ was held on the evening of Sunday, May 20, 1962. The featured organist was Edmund Sereno Ender, organist and choirmaster of St. Thomas Church, St. Petersburg, Florida. The program provided a short biographical sketch: "…was born in New Haven, Conn., and studied music at Yale University. He also studied in Germany and England and has held professorships in several colleges.

Previous to his retirement he was organist and choirmaster at Old St. Paul's Church, Baltimore, Md., and was a member of the faculties of Goucher College and the Peabody Conservatory of Music."

Mr. Ender played the following program:

Concert Overture	Maitland
Nocturne	King-Miller
Will o' the Wisp	Nevin
Paean	Matthews
Fugue in C minor	Bach
Fantaisie Dialoguee	Boellmann
Canon in B minor	Schumann
Finlandia	Sebelius (sic)
Roulade	Bingham
In Springtime	Kinder
Toccata (from the Fifth Symphony)	Widor

The four manual console of the Toledo Pipe Organ Comp. instrument at St. John's. This photo was taken by the author August 1977. Notice the "heavy duty" power buttons to the lef. the Pedal and Swell stop jams. One button turned the blower and off but the second one had no apparent use. (Photo author)

The TPOC organ provided good service for St. John's from 1962-1997. Church services at the time were on Sunday morning at 8:00 a.m. and 10:30 a.m. Special services such as Lent and Advent, weddings, funerals, ordinations, the 100th Anniversary Celebration (1964), and a 1976 American Bi-centennial Concert of combined choirs from the Bellevue area churches, all availed themselves, to one extent or another, the use of the TPOC.

By the time the Centennial Celebration of 1964 was held, St. John's was blessed with and enjoying the talents of two organists, Mrs. Roland (Grace) Morris, the senior organist, and Mrs. Theodore (Marlene) Buck, the assistant organist. Marlene Buck played the 8:00 a.m. Sunday services while Grace Morris played the 10:30 a.m. services. Centennial Sunday was celebrated on June 7, 1964, while Centennial Homecoming Sunday was celebrated on June 14, 1964. The organ played a significant role in both Sunday celebrations. Information on these services does not provide the names of the preludes and postludes used. I will summarize the musical parts of both services:

Centennial Sunday, June 7, 1964: Hymns used at both the 8:00 and 10:30 a.m. services.
    Hymn: *The Church's One Foundation*
    Hymn: *Glorious Things of Thee Are Spoken*
    Sermon: "What's Going on Around Here?" Reverend R. Van Scoy
    Anthem (8:00 a.m.) "The Song of Praise" Children's Choir
        Mrs. R. Donald Paul, Director; Mrs. Gerald Sweigard, Piano
    Anthem (10:30 a.m.) "Praise Ye the Lord" Combined Senior and Youth Choirs
        Mr. Robert Leckrone-Director, Mrs. Grace Morris-Organ
            Miss Barbara Hunt-Piano
    The Doxology
    Hymn: *Now Thank We All Our God*

Centennial Homecoming Sunday, June 14, 1964: Hymns were used at both the 8:00 and 10:30 a.m. services.
    Hymn: *When Morning Guilds the Skies*
    Hymn: *What A Friend We Have in Jesus*
    Sermon: Reverend Paul Rempe
    Anthem (8:00 AM): "Praise the Lord" The Youth Choir
        Mr. Robert Leckrone-Director, Miss Barbara Hunt, Piano
    Anthem (10:30): "Hallelujah" (Psalm 150) the Senior Choir
        Mr. Robert Leckrone-Director, Mrs. Morris-Organ
    Hymn: *Stand Up, Stand Up for Jesus*

On Wednesday, June 10, 1964, St. John's hosted The Centennial Lawn-Fette Celebration, an old-fashioned lawn social and the entire Bellevue community was invited. Homemade ice cream and sandwiches, strawberries, and assorted beverages were the fare of the evening. Music was provided by "The Bellevue Barber Shoppers" and "The Girl Choraliers." A good time was had by all.

No changes to the TPOC organ's specification were made until 1993, when my family approached St. John's about the possible installation of a Great to Great 4' coupler in memory of Paul's parents, Paul R. and Ruth D. Lieber. A presentation at the September 29, 1993, council meeting by the author explained the addition of the Great 4'. Council approved the change to the organ. This facilitated the removal of the 4' Clarion draw knob on the Great. The 4' Clarion could be coupled from the Solo division so there was no loss of its use. Julian Bulley installed the Great to Great 4' coupler on the organ during the winter of 1994.

With the advent of the 1990s, the organ started to display symptoms of wear and just being tired. In discussions between Julian Bulley and myself, Bulley informed me that the organ needed a re-leathering at a cost of approximately $40,000. At the November 18, 1993, council meeting, discussions on "organ repairs (leathers)" took place. It was "suggested that an article be put in the newsletter concerning this so that memorials can be given to the organ fund."

Knowing several of the outstanding problems facing the organ, I consulted with The Reverend Frank Stoldt, church organist Marlene Buck, Pastor David Wietelmann, and the congregational council. At the annual Congregational Meeting, November 19,1995, a motion by Marlene Buck, organist, and seconded by Delmar Koch to establish an Organ Renovation Committee was approved. Congregational President Steve Young appointed the following members: Paul Lieber, Chair, Marlene Buck, Kay Dubbert, Delmar Koch, Milt Zimmerman, Earl Koch, Elizabeth Burr, and Gertrude Hammersmith. Later, three additional members of the committee would be added: Charlotte Zimmerman, Robert Dubbert, and Donald Reiderman. This committee was tasked with approaching other builders for their opinion and estimates of cost to bring the organ into first class shape. The Schantz Organ Company of Orrville, Ohio and the Bunn Minnick Pipe Organ Company of Columbus, Ohio, had been asked to independently inspect the instrument and then submit their recommendations. Both companies were given carte blanche to design a new instrument, with the understanding that the 16' Tuba (Trombone) rank and the 16' Double Open Diapason (Wood Open) be retained.

During the summer of 1994, I toured both the Bunn Minnick Pipe Organ Company facilities (July) and those of the Schantz Organ Company (August). Both facilities were impressive and the administrators and employees of both companies' cordial and knowledgeable. While at the respective facilities, I sat down with the leadership of both firms and discussed the possible renovation of the TPOC instrument at St. John's Lutheran Church.

In a letter dated November 3, 1994, the Schantz Organ Company reported the findings of their inspection of the organ, which they feared the church would find "rather severe." Quoting from the letter:

"Dear Paul:

We must apologize for taking so long to get a letter to you following visits by Burton Tidwell and Tom Mierau to review the present instrument at your church. This fall has been rather busy for us, and we have struggled with exactly how to approach an organ project for your church. After reviews of the instrument, we fear that you may find our recommendation rather severe.

The mechanical survey of the organ indicates that the condition of the instrument is not good. The mechanism of the Moller chests is very sensitive to extremes of temperature and humidity and is becoming increasingly unreliable. Tom (Mierau) indicates that you have verified this as a problem. This is due to the design of the chests. The primary action is located outside the wind chest and is connected by tubing. Moller abandoned this design years ago for obvious reasons. We feel that rebuilding these chests as they are would only perpetuate a problematic design. Any attempts to modify the design would be nearly as expensive as entirely new chests.

Once a project has reached the level of requiring new chests, we feel that an honest appraisal of the tonal design is critical. If the design is good, it is certainly good stewardship of the resources to retain a great deal, if not all of the pipework. If the design is not good, perhaps it is best to consider a modified design.

Burton (Tidwell) has indicated that while there are several individual sounds in the organ that are nice, the physical configuration of the instrument coupled with the overall tonal design do not

30

yield a musical result worthy of a strict preservation of this instrument. Therefore, our recommendation would be to pursue this project as basically a new instrument in which we would make every effort to retain as many ranks of pipes of the present instrument as possible for incorporation into the new organ's design.

It is our hope that you do not find our approach offensive. This instrument is certain to have served your church faithfully for many years. We do not intend to seem inflexible in our willingness to work with you. We simply feel that anything short of this approach would yield a compromised instrument."

After about a year of study by the organ committee, a letter dated November 2, 1995, was sent to Mr. Timothy Mann of Schantz asking for a formal proposal for a four manual, 50-rank pipe organ. Use of the existing instrument or parts thereof was to be at their discretion. It was verbally communicated to Schantz that the 16' Tuba rank the 16' Wood Open rank were to be included in any proposal. The organ committee asked for a complete specification for a 4 manual, 50-rank organ, solid-state console controls, total cost of the proposed pipe organ including installation, etc., terms of payment and warranty, and scheduled delivery date.

On December 1, 1995, Schantz answered our request saying they were delighted to have the opportunity to work with the church on this project. They also asked that their engineer, Mr. Eric Gastier, visit the church to, once again, examine the space available for the new instrument. "After we have reevaluated the space for the layout of our design, we would like to set up a time to meet with you and other interested parties to present out (sic, our) proposal."

Phil Minnick and Victor John of the Bunn Minnick Pipe Organ Company inspected the instrument at St. John's during the late summer of 1994. After consultation between myself, Marlene Buck, Pastor Dave Wietelmann, and the church council, it was decided that Bunn Minnick would take over the care of the organ as of January 1995. Thus, St. John's severed its relationship with Julian Bulley and his pipe organ company, which had earlier moved to Dayton, Ohio. In a letter dated December 14, 1994, Philip Minnick outlined their proposed care of the instrument and enclosed a signed copy of the agreement.

The Bunn Minnick Pipe Organ Company presented their proposal dated October 3, 1995, for a new 50-rank organ to the members of the organ committee. President Philip Minnick and General Manager Victor John gave the presentation which was explained in a detailed written document given to each of the committee members. It reads as follows:

"Since our initial inspection over a year ago, we have had the opportunity to work closely with your pipe organ by performing regular maintenance. We have become very familiar with its positive and negative points.

On the negative side: The organ is getting very tired mechanically. Leather is failing and some mechanical components are just simply wearing out. We do not agree with some of the

Mrs. Lillian Reynolds standing in the leathering room of the Bunn Minnick Pipe Organ Company facility. Mrs. Reynolds was the office manager for the company. She was the first person whom I contacted. Before the author's first meeting with Bunn Minnick officials, Lillian, as she was affectionately known, took me out to lunch at a restaurant of my choice in Columbus. "A lady of the old school", Lillian had great charm, a dry wit, and was a delight to be around. Later in the afternoon I met with Philip Minnick President of the Company and other company employees. (Photo by author)

methods and quality of the actual installation. The condition of the wiring is terrible, and nearly impossible to service. There are some parts of the organ that are inaccessible for making repairs because of the installation. There are many pipes on offset chests that operate from tubing running across the chamber. Some changes should have been made to allow better service. Many pipes are severely dented; nevertheless, they are restorable. The specification is very dated and has a thick heavy sound with many duplications. The organ is dirty, and dirt does affect performance.

For some of the positive points: Even considering the cost differential from 1964 (sic 1961-62) when the organ was installed to the present, you got a sizeable instrument at a very reasonable price. There has been little need for repairs other than tuning. The original Möller pipework was of excellent quality and is worthy of restoration. This existing pipework contains wonderful sounds which can form an exciting basis for a revised instrument. Many original pipes would be considered too costly for inclusion in a new organ if they were not already there. By moving some pipes to new positions and by changing some of the tone qualities by rescaling and re-voicing, we can use all existing ranks and yet eliminate the tonal duplications we criticized above. The console is of high-quality construction and can be retrofitted with state-of-the-art technology. The blower is in very good condition. Existing regulators can be rebuilt and retained. Some existing chests can be modified for reuse. .

Bunn Minnick offers solutions: When the original organ was designed nearly seventy years ago, the primary organ literature was performance of Wagnerian opera scores. Choruses of sounds which had existed through the previous centuries of organ tonal design were all but eliminated in favor of numerous orchestral sounds. This left an organ specification that could imitate the orchestra but did little for encouraging exciting congregational singing. After this period of American organ design, which lasted from 1900 to 1930, the pendulum swung far to the left. At that point the new trend created exaggerated pseudo copies of historic organs, which were void of the lush sounds and full of screechy, harsh tones. That extreme trend has fortunately passed.

We believe that the best pipe organ today is a combination of styles. Our concept is based on century-old designs beginning with the Principal Chorus and augmented with orchestral colors such as those found in your present organ. This allows effective and exciting performance of all styles of literature. This pipe organ will further encourage exciting congregational singing.

The many orchestral strings, the oboe, clarinet, trombone (sic, tuba), and flutes presently in your organ cannot be duplicated without great expense. They are often considered luxury items in a new organ. ***These must be kept!*** By Judiciously adding a clean principal chorus (basic historic organ tone), adding complimentary reed tones, and by reworking some existing pipes to provide additional colors, we can create for you an instrument which will inspire worshipers far into the next century.

It is possible that the question of cost alone could preempt further discussion. A quality pipe organ represents good stewardship. Some persons may say there will be a lower cost with the purchase of an electronic substitute. This is simply not true. When considering this, remember that the average life expectancy of an electronic is only 25 years. Good stewardship comes from retaining the existing organ as a basis. In the long run it will cost less. But we must ***not*** look at cost only..."

Bunn Minnick proposed a four manual, 50-rank, 3,138 total pipes, seven ranks extending to 16' pipe organ for St. John's Lutheran, Bellevue. In their proposal they stated that parts of all 36 ranks (2,277 pipes) would be retained as the basis for the new organ. Seventy-six pipes would not be incorporated into the new instrument. Eight hundred seventy-three pipes would be added by Bunn Minnick, 14 ranks in all, at a total cost of $224,953.00. Their proposed specification is as follows:

Great (visually exposed)

16 Contra Gemshorn	Rank 1	73 existing pipes (1-12 Ped 16 Violone; 13-73 Gt 8 Gemshorn)
8 Prinzipal	Rank 2	61 pipes by Bunn Minnick
8 Holz Gedeckt	Rank 3	73 existing pipes (Sw 8 Gedeckt)
8 Gemshorn (enclosed)		from rank #1
8 Unda Maris II (Choir)		from ranks #16 & #17
4 Oktav	Rank 4	73 pipes by Bunn Minnick
4 Halb Gedeckt		from rank #3
2 2/3 Quinte	Rank 5	61 pipes: 1-24 existing (Gt III Mixture); 25-61 by Bunn Minnick
2 Klein Octav		from rank #4
III Mixtur	Ranks 6-8	183 existing pipes rescaled (Gt III Mixture, plus misc. top notes) [1 1/3']
II Zymbel	Ranks 9-10	122 pipes Bunn Minnick (1/2')
16 Contra Trumpet (enc)		from rank #12
8 Trompette Heroïque	Rank 11	73 pipes by Bunn Minnick
8 Trumpet (enc)	Rank 12	73 existing pipes (1-61 Sw 8 Cornopean; 62-73 Sw 8 Diapason)

8 Clarinet (Choir)		from rank #23
4 Clarion (enc)		from rank #12
Great Unison Off		
4 Great to Great		

Choir (enclosed)

16 Contra Dulciana		from rank #37 & 13-61 from rank #16
8 Geigen Principal	Rank 13	61 existing pipes (1-12 Ch 8 Diapason; 13-61 Gt 4 Octave)
8 Concert Flute	Rank 14	61 existing pipes (Sw 8 Flute Traverso)
8 Flute Celeste tc	Rank 15	49 existing pipes (Gt 8 Melodia)
8 Dulciana	Rank 16	61 existing pipes (Ch 8 Dulciana)
8 Unda Maris tc	Rank 17	49 existing pipes (Ch 8 Unda Maris)
4 Prinzipal	Rank 18	61 pipes by Bunn Minnick
4 Lieblich Flöte	Rank 19	73 pipes existing (Ch 4 Flute d' Amour)
2 2/3 Nasat	Rank 20	61 existing pipes rescaled (Sw 8 Aeoline)
2 Flöte		from rank #19
1 3/5 Terz	Rank 21	61 existing pipes rescaled (Sw 2 Flautino)
1 1/3 Klein Nasat		from rank #20
1 Fugara	Rank 22	61 existing pipes rescaled (Sw 1 3/5 of III Dolce Cornet)
8 Trompette Heroïque		from rank #11
8 Trumpet (Great)		from rank #12
8 Clarinet	Rank 23	61 existing pipes (Ch 8 Clarinet)
Zimbelstern		prepared
Tremulant		by Bunn Minnick
16 Choir to Choir		
Choir Unison Off		
4 Choir to Choir		

Swell (enclosed)

16 Bourdon Doux	Rank 24	73 existing pipes (Sw 16 Bourdon)
8 Montre	Rank 25	61 existing pipes (Sw 8 Diapason)
8 Bourdon		from rank #24
8 Gamba	Rank 26	61 existing pipes (Ch 8 Gamba)
8 Voix Celeste	Rank 27	49 existing pipes (Sw 8 Voix Celeste)
4 Prestant	Rank 28	73 existing pipes (Sw 4 Principal)
4 Flute Harmonique	Rank 29	61 existing pipes (Gt 4 Flute)
2 Doublette		from rank #28
IV Plein Jeu	Rank 30-33	244 pipes by Bunn Minnick (1')
16 Contre Trompette	Rank 34	85 pipes by Bunn Minnick
8 Trompette Heroïque		from rank #11
8 Trompette		from rank #34
8 Basson	Rank 35	61 existing pipes (Sw Oboe)
8 Vox Humana	Rank 36	61 existing pipes (Sw 8 Vox Humana)
4 Clairon		from rank #34

| | | Tremulant | by Bunn Minnick |
| 16 Swell to Swell |
| Swell Unison Off |
| 4 Swell to Swell |

Solo (enclosed with Choir)

16 Quintadena	Rank 37	73 existing pipes (Gt 16 Quintadena)
8 Stentorphone	Rank 38	61 existing pipes (So 8 Diapason)
8 Gross Flute	Rank 39	61 existing pipes (So 8 Major Flute)
8 Quintadena		from rank #37
8 Viol d' Orchestra	Rank 40	61 existing pipes (So 8 Gross Gamba)
8 Viole Celeste	Rank 41	61 existing pipes (Sw 8 Viole)
4 Zauberflöte	Rank 42	61 existing pipes (Gt 8 Diapason)
2 2/3 Nazard	Rank 43	61 pipes Bunn Minnick
2 Piccolo	Rank 44	61 existing pipes (Ch 8 Concert Flute)
1 3/5 Tierce	Rank 45	61 existing pipes rescaled (Sw 2 2/3 of III Cornet + 1 top note)
16 Grande Cornet VII		composite by Bunn Minnick (16, 8, 4, 2 2/3, 2, 1 3/5, 1 1/7)
16 Trompette Heroïque		from rank #11
16 Trombone	Rank 46	85 existing pipes (So 16 Trombone)
8 Trompette Heroïque		from rank #11
8 Tromba		from rank #46
4 Trompette Heroïque		from rank #11
4 Tromba Clarion		from rank #46
Chimes		existing
Tremulant		by Bunn Minnick

| 16 Solo to Solo |
| Solo Unison Off |
| 4 Solo to Solo |

Pedal

32 Grand Harmonics		composite by Bunn Minnick
32 Contra Bass		resultant from rank #47
32 Echo Bourdon		resultant from rank #24
16 Wood Diapason	Rank 47	44 existing pipes (1-32 Ped Diapason, 33-44 Ch 8 Con Flute 13-24)
16 Subbass	Rank 48	56 existing pipes (Ped 16 Bourdon)
16 Contra Gemshorn (Great)		from rank 1
16 Quintadena		from rank #37
16 Bourdon Doux		from rank #24
8 Principal	Rank 49	68 existing pipes (1-12 Gt 8 Diapason, 13-68 Ch 8 Diapason)
8 Major Flute		from rank #47
8 Bass Flute		from rank #48
8 Gemshorn (Great)		from rank #1

8 Bourdon (Swell)		from rank #24
5 1/3 Quinte (Swell)		from rank #24
4 Octave		from rank #49
4 Flute		from rank #48
2 Super Octave		from rank #49
III Rauschpfeife	Rank 50	44 pipes (2 2/3 + 1 1/3) by Bunn Minnick and from rank #52
32 Contra Trombone		1-12 electronic; 13-32 from rank #46
16 Trombone		from rank #46
16 Contre Trompette		from rank #34
8 Trompette Heroïque		from rank #11
8 Tromba		from rank #46
8 Trompette		from rank #34
4 Tromba Clarion		from rank #46
4 Clarinet		from rank #23

(This stop was added later at the behest of Rev. Frank Stoldt)

Couplers (located on nameboard)

8 Great to Pedal	16 Swell to Great	8 Solo to Swell
4 Great to Pedal	8 Swell to Great	
8 Swell to Pedal	4 Swell to Great	8 Swell to Solo
4 Swell to Pedal	16 Choir to Great	
8 Choir to Pedal	8 Choir to Great	8 Great to Choir
4 Choir to Pedal	4 Choir to Great	16 Swell to Choir
8 Solo to Pedal	16 Solo to Great	8 Swell to Choir
4 Solo to Pedal	8 Solo to Great	4 Swell to Choir
	4 Solo to Great	8 Solo to Choir

Four Manual Console Details

Existing four manual console will be retrofitted as follows:
>   All electric action will be provided; Draw knob style stop control.
>   Sufficient cable will be provided for the console to be movable.
>   Bunn Minnick Solid State Coupler Action will be provided.
>   Lighted plexiglass music rack; Pedal Light; Digital clock.

Solid State Capture Combination Action:
>   10 Levels of Memory; Lock for Levels 1-5; 18 General Pistons.
>   10 Duplicate General Toe Studs; General Cancel Piston; Set Piston.
>   6 Great, Swell, Choir, Solo, and Pedal Pistons; 6 Duplicate Pedal Toe
>   Pistons; Cancel Piston for Each Division.

>   Sforzando Reversible, Piston and Toe Stud; Tutti Reversible, Piston and
>   Toe Stud; Great to Pedal Reversible, Piston and Toe Stud; Swell to Pedal
>   Reversible, Piston and Toe Stud; Choir to Pedal Reversible, Piston and
>   Toe Stud; Solo to Pedal Reversible, Piston and Toe Stud; Zimbelstern
>   Reversible, Piston and Toe Stud.
>   32 Grand Harmonics Reversible, Piston and Toe Stud.

36

32 Contrabass Reversible, Piston and Toe Stud.
32 Echo Bourdon Reversible, Piston and Toe Stud.
32 Contra Trombone Reversible, Piston and Toe Stud.

Sforzando Indicator Light; Signal Indicator Light; Tutti Indicator Light; Crescendo Pedal; Four Crescendo Indicator Lights; Current Indicator Light; Signal Button; Swell, Choir, and Solo Expression Pedals.

With the Bunn Minnick proposal for a 50-rank instrument in hand, the organ committee waited for Schantz to present its proposal with the requirement that both the 16' Tuba (Trombone) rank and the 16' Wood Open rank be retained. In the late winter of 1996 Timothy Mann met with the organ committee and presented the Schantz proposal. Total cost of the Schantz proposal was $416,210. Of the TPOC organ, Schantz would re-use only 437 pipes.

Schantz Recommendation For a 50 Rank Organ, St. John's Lutheran, Bellevue, Ohio 44811

Great: 12 ranks, 744 pipes (134 exposed)

16 Violone---73 pipes
8 Principal---61 pipes
8 Rohrflute---61 pipes
8 Violone (from 16)
4 Octave---61 pipes
4 Hohlflöte---61 pipes

2 2/3 Nasat---61 pipes
2 Blockflöte---61 pipes
1 3/5 Tierce---61 pipes
IV Mixture---244 pipes (1 1/3')
8 Festival Trumpet (Choir)

Swell: 15 ranks, 939 pipes

16 Bourdon---73 pipes
8 Geigenprincipal---61 pipes
8 Bourdon (from 16)
8 Salicional---61 pipes
8 Voix Celeste---61 pipes
4 Principal---61 pipes
4 Traversflöte---61 pipes
2 2/3 Nasard---61 pipes

2 Gemshorn---61 pipes
IV Plein Jeu---244 pipes (2')
16 Basson-Hautbois---73 pipes
8 Festival Trumpet (Choir)
8 Trompette---61 pipes
8 Hautbois (from 16)
4 Clarion---61 pipes

Choir: 13 ranks, 781 pipes

8 Spitzprincipal---61 pipes
8 Gedackt---61 pipes
8 Flauto Dolce---61 pipes
8 Flauto Celeste, tc---49 pipes
4 Principal---61 pipes
4 Koppelflöte---61 pipes
2 Octave (from IV Mixture)
1 1/3 Quinteflöte---61 pipes
IV Mixture---244 pipes (1')
8 Festival Trumpet 61 pipes

Bombarde: 3 ranks, 183 pipes

8 Harmonic Flute---61 pipes
16 Festival Trumpet, tc (Choir)
16 Dulzian---61 pipes
8 Festival Trumpet (Choir)
8 Trumpet---61 pipes

8 Krummhorn---61 pipes

Pedal: 6 ranks, 260 pipes

32 Resultant	8 Bourdon (Swell)
16 Principal---44 pipes (1-12 existing)	8 Choralbass---32 pipes
16 Subbass---32 pipes	4 Spitzflöte (from 8)
16 Violone (Great)	II Mixture---64 pipes
16 Bourdon (Swell)	16 Posaune---44 pipes
8 Octave (from 16 Principal)	16 Basson (Swell)
8 Spitzflöte---44 pipes	8 Festival Trumpet (Choir)
8 Violone (Great)	8 Posaune (from 16))
	4 Hautbois (Swell)

After Timothy Mann's presentation, questions immediately arose about not retaining the 16' Tuba (Trombone) and 16' Wood Open ranks since the committee had made it quite clear that those ranks were to be retained in any proposal submitted by Schantz. Mann calmly explained that there was no place for these two ranks in the proposal by their tonal director, Burton Tidwell. Tidwell's, meaning the Schantz Organ Company's tonal concepts would not allow for their use. After fielding questions about the cost of Schantz's proposal, Mr. Mann was thanked for his time and his excellent presentation, after which the committee adjourned.

Based on the preface to their proposal, Schantz did not fundamentally believe in retaining much of the instrument, citing a lack of effective scaling and tonal quality. "Our tonal director, Mr. Burton K. Tidwell, has reviewed the instrument. While there are several individual sounds that are very effective, the scaling and voicing of many of the ranks of pipes in the instrument do not contribute to a total that is capable of effectively leading a congregation in song or performing a broad cross of organ literature," Schantz argued.

Over the next few weeks, the organ committee compared and discussed both proposals. The committee was not pleased that its only request/requirement to Schantz had been the retention of the 16' Tuba and 16' Wood Open ranks and that Schantz refused to comply, while at the same time Bunn Minnick enthusiastically agreed that the two ranks would and should be incorporated into the new organ. The cost to duplicate these two ranks in any new organ would be prohibitive for most churches so to the committee's amazement and disappointment, Schantz was going to relegate them to the "tonal trash heap". Schantz's intransigence on this point damaged its chances of having their proposal accepted.

Next came the discussion on just how much both companies retained pipe work, chests, and retention of the Möller four manual console. Although carte blanche had been given to both companies on the pipework (ranks), Bunn Minnick's proposal kept the vast majority of the TPOC organ's pipework, arguing they could meld it into a cohesive instrument through re-voicing and rank placement with the addition of 14 new ranks. The Schantz Organ Company used only 437 pipes from the TPOC organ and added 42 new ranks of Schantz pipework to the organ they proposed. Of the 16' ranks in the TPOC instrument, Bunn Minnick used all of them, while Schantz used just one complete rank, plus pipes 1-24 of the existing Swell 16' Bourdon, and 1-12 existing pipes from the 16' Violone. Sixteen-foot ranks are costly to replace. The committee determined the massive cost differential of $191,257 between the two bids largely was the result of Schantz not retaining all 16' ranks, not using more of the TPOC organ's pipe work, and not refurbishing some of the existing chests as Bunn Minnick planned to do. Also, the TPOC four manual Möller console became a sticking point. Bunn Minnick would retrofit the console for a new instrument, but Schantz had not decided on its use at the time of their presentation to the committee. By using the oak shell of the Möller console it was estimated that St. John's would save several thousand dollars.

Warranty was a concern as well. Bunn Minnick offered a 10-year warranty on materials and labor, whereas Schantz offered a five-year warranty on materials and labor.

As noted in the May 1996 monthly newsletter, "On Saturday, March 9, 1996, several members of the organ committee travelled to Columbus to tour and inspect the facilities of the Bunn Minnick Pipe Organ Company. Philip Minnick, president of Bunn Minnick, led a tour of the plant and every aspect of building a pipe organ was explained in detail…We observed Bunn Minnick employees at their workstations carrying out the following: wiring of a new console and pipe chests; the refurbishing, cleaning, and voicing of pipes; the building of chests and consoles in Bunn Minnick's woodshop; and the re-leathering of a chest." After the tour committee members and company employees enjoyed a luncheon where committee members could interact with the employees.

At the May 30, 1996, church council meeting, I gave a presentation of the organ committee's findings and recommendation. After the presentation, the church council decided on a plan to move forward. A meeting open to all congregational members would be held in the Fellowship Hall on Sunday, June 16, 1996, between services for anyone who wished to know more about the organ renovation or to ask questions pertaining to it. Also, a motion was made by Gale Burke and seconded by Evelyn Woodruff that a congregational meeting would be held on Saturday, June 22, and Sunday, June 23, to vote on the organ committee's recommendation and, if the congregation approved, envelopes should be placed in the pews to garner donations for the upcoming organ project. The motion passed.

At the June 22 and June 23 congregational meetings, the members voted overwhelmingly in favor of the committee's recommendation that The Bunn Minnick Pipe Organ Company of Columbus, Ohio renovate the organ by a vote of 193-12.

At the June 28, 1996, church council meeting, a report was given on the ballot results for the organ renovation. A discussion ensued concerning raising the needed funds for the project. Milt Zimmerman recommended that the church borrow the necessary funds from the First National Bank of Bellevue to ensure a start date from Bunn Minnick of June 1997. The loan would be paid off as monies came into the organ fund. A motion to accept Zimmerman's recommendation that council proceed with borrowing as needed for the organ project if it was in line with the church constitution. The motion was seconded by Evelyn Woodruff. The motion carried.

Bunn Minnick's payment plan called for 50 percent of the total cost of the project to be paid to get on its calendar for a start date. There was to be an additional payment of 25 percent at the time of dismantling the organ and transporting it to company's facilities in Columbus. The final 25 percent was to be paid upon installation and completion of the job. So, on July 16, 1996, in the presence of the organ renovation committee members, a check in the amount of $112,476.50 was given to Bunn Minnick's general manager, Victor John.

During the summer of 1996, the organ committee moved quickly to develop plans to garner the needed funds for the renovation and expansion of the organ. The financial chair of the organ committee was Milton Zimmerman. Although St. John's had secured a four-year loan from the First National Bank, Zimmerman lost no time in organizing and launching the fundraising campaign. Initially dinners/meetings were held at the Zimmerman residence to lay out the financial campaign's strategy. These meetings were attended by additional members of the congregation. Charlotte Zimmerman and several ladies of the church prepared city chicken dinners for all in attendance. A card system was developed. The meeting attendees were each given several cards with the names of congregational members on them. Thus, the attendees would be responsible for canvassing the named members on the cards in their possession. By using this system, all members of the congregation were approached to financially support the organ project. Also, some local businesses, residents, and non-residents of Bellevue who were not formally associated with St. John's Lutheran pledged financial support as well. The financial campaign was so successful that the loan for the organ project was paid off 11 months ahead of its due date.

The Bunn Minnick Era (1997-2017)

Elizabeth Birr and Alice Stoldt (seated) helping Phil Minnick disassemble the Möller console for shipment back to the Bunn Minnick facility where it will be retrofitted and expanded. (Photo courtesy of Marlene Buck)

Late June 1997 saw the TPOC organ removed from St. John's. Before the removal process could move forward, the financial chair of the organ committee, Milton Zimmerman was brought up to the choir loft in a wheelchair for what ultimately would be his last time to hear the organ. Milt had been in failing health and came straight to the church after being discharged from The Bellevue Hospital. Marlene Buck swung into "God Bless America" and then I played The Ohio State University's alma mater (Milt was a graduate of OSU and a huge Buckeyes fan). Unfortunately, Milt passed away in February 1998, one month before the organ was partially re-installed at St. John's.

Along with the employees of the Bunn Minnick Pipe Organ Company, many members of the congregation helped in the removal process. The organ project benefitted the congregation of St. John's Lutheran in many ways. First, we were getting an enlarged and reconditioned pipe organ. Second, the congregation pulled together and met the financial burden head-on. Third, and most important, the project sparked a deeper fellowship and spirit of cooperation among the church's membership. During both the removal and the return of the organ, church members took an active hand in dismantling the organ, loading when it was removed and unloading when the organ returned, cleaning and painting the pipe chamber.

Brenda Manasco looks on as a pipe from the 16' Wood Open rank is carried down the fire escape stairs by Ed Moyer (middle white hat) and me (top). Delmar Koch steadies the pipe and prepares to help carry it to the truck for loading. (Photo courtesy of Marlene Buck)

41

Ed Moyer (red shirt) and Ted Buck (standing on lift) load a reed rank into the waiting arms of Robert Peacock, an unknown Bunn Minnick employee, and Bud Kryling (red hat) for the trip to the Bunn Minnick facilities in Columbus, Ohio. (Photo courtesy of Marlene Buck)

Delmar Koch walking past a row of 16' Wood Open pipes as they are prepared to be loaded into a truck for transport to the Bunn Minnick facility in Columbus. (Photo courtesy of Marlene Buck)

Several members travelled to Columbus on a couple of Saturdays to give Bunn Minnick employees a hand in moving the project forward. The women of the church cooked meals for both Bunn Minnick and congregational workers particularly during the re-installation of the organ (the cuisine was a good deal tastier than eating at the local fast-food establishments).

Electrical and construction needs for the placement of the new instrument were the responsibility of the parish. With the removal of the TPOC organ, major structural changes/additions had to be made at the rear of the church to support the new exposed Great division that the previous instrument lacked. Under the leadership of Greg Zimmerman and with the guidance of structural engineer Tom Ruppert of Thomas Steel, Zimmerman Construction welded three steel I-beams, purchased from Thomas Steel, to the steel supports in the rear wall of the church. Along with the three I-beams, they constructed the platform necessary to the weight of the chests, reservoirs, and pipes of the new exposed Great division.

An employee from the Zimmerman Construction Company working on the structural addition to St. John's choir loft. The three holes in the ceiling are where the three steel beams from Thomas Steel, a local steel fabricating company, were welded into the existing structure to support the new exposed Great division, which can be seen in front of the support pillars. (Photo by author)

All the TPOC organ was removed and transported to Bunn Minnick's facility in Columbus, with one exception. The bottom seven pipes of the 16 Wood Open (Diapason) remained at St. John's. In later years, St. John's would have trouble keeping the bottom three pipes regulated and in tune. These seven pipes should have been taken back to Columbus to be cleaned, washed, checked for wind leaks and re-glued if necessary. When I asked Phil Minnick why the pipes were left in Bellevue, he said that Bunn Minnick did not have a truck large enough to transport them back to Columbus. Minnick told me that the bottom seven pipes could be cleaned up and washed on site, so there was no need to take them to Columbus. This was a mistake pure and simple. The bottom seven of this rank should have been taken back to the Bunn Minnick facility to check for wind leaks and/or if the seams needed to be re-glued, where they had the wherewithal to make any necessary adjustments and possible repairs. The 16 Wood Diapason is buried in the rear of the Choir division. In the event we must extricate any of these seven pipes, most of the Choir division would have to be removed.

Members of the Bellevue Redmen football, wrestling, track, and baseball teams aided in moving, cleaning, and washing these large and heavy pipes.

Bellevue High School athletes pose with the bottom seven pipes of the 16' Wood Diapason after they cleaned and washed them in the Choir chamber. Right to left, Nate Goebbel, Matt De Polo, Rob Gonzales (kneeling) Craig Jarrett, Laramie Spurlock, Kit Ruffing, Jason Haughawout, Pete Lepley (leaning on pipe), Mark Sloesser, and Rich Felske. (Photo by author)

Meanwhile, Bunn Minnick had a deadline to meet by completing the contracted work on the organ, the organ's expansion, and its re-installation in playable condition by the April 1998 Easter services at St. John's.

During the late summer and early fall of 1997, members of St. John's Congregation would travel to the Bunn Minnick facilities in Columbus, Ohio to lend a hand with and work on non-technical jobs to move the project along. Pictured in the Bunn Minnick leathering room are Bud Kryling, Lennie Bowers, and Delmar Koch. (Photo by author)

On occasion, fellow parishioners and I travelled to the Bunn Minnick facilities in Columbus to check the progress of the project. An article in St. John's January monthly newsletter makes that point:

> "On Saturday, January 17,1998 Bob and Ellen Dubbert and Paul Lieber inspected the progress made on our pipe organ. The Choir division is in the erecting room completely assembled and playable…A couple of organists from the Bunn Minnick staff and Paul Lieber played the Choir for a little over an hour. All the pipework for the Choir division has been completed and voiced. The majority of the new pipework has arrived. Although there is still a good deal of work to conclude, unofficially February-March 1998 appears to be when Bunn Minnick will install the organ."

During the period June 1997-March 1998 additions were made to the organ's specification in the form of gifts to the congregation. First, The Reverend Frank Stoldt donated the cost of the new Zimbelstern to be added to the organ. Second, an E.M. Skinner 8' French Horn rank was added to the Solo division. The 73 pipes of the French Horn rank and the chests (bottom twelve pipes on offset chest) cost $9,993.00. Funding the 8' French Horn came from several donors: Mrs. Elizabeth Hill Johnson, Greg and Carol Zimmerman, Delmar and Georgine Koch, and Paul and Karen Lieber.

Bunn Minnick also made an addition to the specification in memory of Milton Zimmerman, the financial chair of the organ committee, whose' health declined to the point he passed away before the organ was re-installed. Bunn Minnick's letter of June 13, 1998, to his wife Charlotte follows:

Dear Charlotte:

Words cannot adequately express our gratitude for all that you, Milt, and your family did to make the organ project a beautiful success. Your family's skill ranged from fund raising, construction work, fellowship, fantastic meals that were prepared, as well as so much more.

We know that none of this could have happened without prayer, belief in the project, and hours of hard work. Per the contract specifications, we had planned to use an electronic unit to synthesize twelve bass notes of 32' pitch which we felt were needed tonally in the organ's ensemble. Because of space and cost considerations, most pipe organs only go to 16' pitch.

I am sure very few, if any, pipe organs in your area have any actual ranks which extend to the 32' pitch range. As we got further into the project, we began thinking that for the scope and magnificence of your pipe organ, it was almost mandatory for us to use real 32' organ pipes.

Since your pipe organ was already going to be exceptional, this was a logical artistic conclusion.

As we began seriously considering this, Milt's health began deteriorating. We had hoped Milt would have been able to hear this addition, but unfortunately time did not allow.

Milt was, and always will be, a tremendous inspiration to us! Therefore, if you will allow, Bob, Leo, and I, wish to give the 32' Contre Bombarde as a tribute to Milt.

I am sorry that Milt could not see the finished project of his work here on earth, but I am certain that he is watching and listening from above.

We are honored to have worked with all of you on this project to the glory of God.

Sincerely,
Philip D. Minnick, President
Bunn Minnick Pipe Organs
CC: Paul Lieber, Organ Committee Chair

Photo of Phil Minnick, President of the Bunn Minnick Pipe Organ Company, with Milton Zimmerman, the financial chair of St. John's Organ Committee, at the Bunn Minnick facility in Columbus, Ohio. (Photo by author)

During the late summer of 2004, as curator of St. John's organ, I requested that Bunn Minnick provide St. John's with a hardcopy of the production specifications for the organ. After some initial wavering on Bunn Minnick's part, I received a letter dated October 7, 2004, from Nicholas L. Fink, operations coordinator, and the production specifications for our organ (Revised 10/15/97-Job #9607). This included all rank details, revised relay specifications, production pipework details, and production chest details for a 4 manual, 61 rank organ. Included in the specifications, the console was prepared for the addition of an 8' English Horn rank (chest was also prepared) in the Solo and the addition of an Antiphonal division. The Antiphonal division has never been installed (A copy of the production specifications are in possession of Paul Lieber and on file in the church office).

Standard pipe prep of washing, dent removal, repairs, and collars were carried out. They also re-leathered all stoppers. The chests that were to be refurbished and reused were repaired and re-leathered and additional new chests and new reservoirs constructed. The entire organ was re-wired, and a new solid-state system designed. Bunn Minnick also installed new winding throughout. The layout of the organ was a vast improvement over the TPOC set up (For the TPOC instrument, one had to remove pipes to gain access to the Great division to repair or tune). The Bunn Minnick layout of the organ made tuning and repair a great deal easier. The following partial specification of the organ differs from the original proposal (differences in italics)*

Great: (visually exposed) – 6 1/2" wp, 5" wp, & 4" wp

16 Contra Gemshorn	Rank 1	73 pipes; 1-12 on 6 ½ wp; 13-74 on 5" wp

Note: This rank will be exposed inclusive of 8' pitch 1-73- request special preparation instruction before beginning pipe prep

8 Prinzipal	Rank 2	*61 pipes new Schopps; scale 45 – 5" wp*

8 Holz Gedeckt	Rank 3	73 pipes; 5" wp

Original Swell Gedeckt – sc 2 ¼ x 1 7/8 @ mid C

Note: This rank will be exposed – request special preparation instructions before beginning pipe prep for this rank

4 Oktav	Rank 4	*61 pipes; 4" wp*

1-61 from BM stock unvoiced McDowell purchase – Schopp to voice – scale 57

2 2/3 Quinte	Rank 5	61 pipes; 4" wp

1-61 original Great III Mixture – 2 2/3 – sc 67/68

2 Klein Oktav	*Rank 6*	*61 pipes; 4" wp; 1-49 original Great III mixture;*

50-61 new Schopp – spotted sc 62; in original proposal 2' borrowed from 4' Oktav

III Mixtur	*Rank 7-9*	*183 pipes – 4" wp - new Schopp – 1 1/3'*

in original proposal 183 existing pipes rescaled + misc top notes

II Zymbel	Rank 10-11	122 pipes – 4" wp – new Schopp
8 Trompette Héroique	Rank 12	73 pipes – 5" wp – new Schopp

Choir: (enclosed) – 4 ½" wp

8 Geigen Principal	Rank 13	*61 pipes – 1-61 original Ch 8 Diapason*
8 Concert Flute	Rank 14	*61 pipes; 1-61 original Gt 8 Melodia*
8 Flute Celeste (tc)	Rank 15	*49 pipes; 13-16 original Sw 8 Flute Traverso*
8 Dulciana	Rank 16	61 pipes; original Ch 8 Dulciana
8 Unda Maris	Rank 17	49 pipes; 13-61 original Ch 8 Unda Maris
4 Prinzipal	Rank 18	61 pipes; BM stock – spotted – sc 59
4 Lieblich Flöte	Rank 19	73 pipes; 1-73 original Ch 4 Flute d' Amour
2 2/3 Nasat	Rank 20	61 pipes; 1-61 original Sw 8 Aeoline rescaled
1 3/5 Terz	Rank 21	*61 pipes; 1-61 original pipes rescaled*

by BM (III Dolce Cornet 2 2/3' rescaled to sc 69/70)

1 Fugara	Rank 22	*49 pipes; from old III Mixture & Schopp*
8 Trumpet	Rank 23	73 pipes; 1-61 original Sw 8 Cornopean;

62-73 from BM stock; solder torn scrolls and cut new; sc 5 ½"; original proposal had this rank on Great but enclosed

8 Clarinet	Rank 24	61 pipes – original Ch 8 Clarinet

Swell: (enclosed) – 4" wp; 73 note

16 Bourdon Doux	Rank 25	*97 pipes; 1-12 stock – 13-73 original*

Sw 16 Bdn 2 ½" x 2 1/16" @ mid C

8 Montre	Rank 26	*73 pipes; 1-73 original Sw 8 Diapason – spotted – sc 45*
8 Gambe	Rank 27	*73 pipes – from BM stock: Trinity Kilgen*

spotted – sc 56; original proposal they stated use of 61 existing Ch 8 Gamba

8 Voix Celeste	*Rank 28*	*73 pipes; 1-73 original Ch 8 Gamba;*

eliminate slots; spotted sc 59; original proposal use 49 existing pipes of Sw 8 Voix Celeste

4 Prestant	Rank 29	73 pipes – from BM stock: 1-12 former Sw Aeoline

rescaled; 13 -73 Brookville 2' Grave Mixture – spotted - - sc 58; original proposal use 73 exisitng pipes of Sw 4 Principal; not industry standard rectified in 2018)

4 Flûte Harmonique	Rank 30	61 pipes; 1-61 original Gt 4' Flute

(Harmonic) spotted sc 58 – arched mouths – sc 75 @ mid C, 1st harmonic

IV Plein Jeu	Rank 31-34	244 pipes; Schopp – 1'
8 Basson	Rank 35	73 pipes; 1-73 original Sw 8 Oboe
8 Vox Humana	Rank 36	73 pipes; 1-61 original Sw 8 Vox Humana
32 Contre Bombarde	*Rank 37*	*97 pipes; 1-97 Schopp; 1-56 Möller from*

Schopp + Schopp ad'l (original proposal called for 1-12 electronic named Contre Trombone with 13-32 from rank #46 So 16 Trombone)

Solo*: (enclosed) – 6 ½" wp – 73 note; add top extension notes from stock if required; Original proposal had Solo and Choir divisions together. During construction at St. John's a wall was erected to separate the two divisions; separate shades for both divisions as well.*

16 Quintadena	Rank 38	85 pipes; 1-85 original Gt 16 Quintadena
8 Stentorphone	Rank 39	73 pipes; 1-73 original So 8 Diapason

lead linen finish – sc 38

8 Gross Flute	Rank 40	73 pipes; 1-73 original So Major Flute

wood – sc 3 1/8" x 8 11/16" @ mid C

8 Viole D' Orchestra	Rank 41	73 pipes; 1-71 original So 8 Gross Gamba
8 Viole Celeste	Rank 42	*73 pipes; 1-73 BM stock Austin*
4 Zauberflöte	Rank 43	*61 pipes; 1-61 BM stock Wurlitzer 8 Concert*

Flute; original proposal used 61 existing pipes Gt 8 Diapason

2 2/3 Nazard	*Rank 44*	*61 pipes; 1-61 original Gt 8 Diapason*

rescaled by BM – 2 notes bigger than 2 2/3 G; BM arched mouths; new sc 58; original proposal used 61 pipes from BM stock

2 Piccolo	*Rank 45*	*61 pipes; 1-61 BM stock – 8 Tibia;*

original proposal called for use of original Ch 8 Concert Flute

1 3/5 Tierce	Rank 46	61 existing pipes; 1-61 original Sw 2 Flautino; sc 68

12" WP for the following:

16 Trombone	Rank 47	85 pipes; 1-85 original Solo 16 Tuba
8 French Horn	Rank 48	(Prepared) ultimately added to Solo
8 English Horn	Rank 49	(Prepared) ultimately added to Solo

*For reasons of brevity, unification, and duplexing, I have not listed the entire rank/stop list. This encompasses all five divisions of the organ. For further details reference pages 33-36

Pedal:

16 Wood Diapason	Rank 50	44 pipes; 1-32 original Ped Diap; 33-44
From BM stock Felgemaker		
16 Subbass	Rank 51	56 pipes; 1-12 Morton + 13-56 BM stock

6 ½" Wp (Solo pressure)

8 Principal   Rank 52   *68 pipes; 1-17 original Gt 8 Diapason; 18-68*
BM stock, Skinner [This tonal error rectified in 2018]; (original proposal called for 1-12 Gt 8
Diapason; 13-68 Ch 8 Diapason from TPOC organ)

III Rauschpfeife   Rank 53   44 pipes (2 2/3 + 1 1/3); 1-61 original Gt 4
Octave – lead – sc 66 @ #1 (original proposal 44 pipes from BM and from rank #52)

Bunn Minnick brought three divisions of the organ back to St. John's on Monday, April 6, 1998, Holy Week. Only the Swell, Choir, and Solo divisions and most of the Pedal division would be installed during Holy Week. It would be the end of May before the Great division was returned and installed. Bunn Minnick employees, congregational members, Bellevue residents, and fortunately Bellevue High School athletes on Spring Break, quickly unloaded the trucks and started the job of re-installation. The athletes were a godsend!

BHS student Kirk Piscitello (left) and Mylan J. Peterson, head of Bunn Minnick's carpentry department, unloading organ parts from a rented truck. (Photo courtesy of Marlene Buck)

From left to right BHS students Rob Gonzales, Scott Miller, Brad Clark (talking with Bunn Minnick employee Karen Freudigman), Ted Buck, and unknown St. John's member, prepare to move the console into the Sanctuary so it can be hoisted into the choir loft. (Photo courtesy of Marlene Buck)

While the trucks were unloaded, the pipes, smaller chests, reservoirs, and the innumerable components that make up a pipe organ were stacked and made ready in the Fellowship Hall. Preparations had been made to hoist the rebuilt console from the floor of the sanctuary up and over the choir loft railing. The scaffolding was set up in the Sanctuary and in the choir loft. Anthony Piscitello, an employee of A. Schulman, Inc., a Bellevue resident, and member of Immaculate Conception Catholic Church, provided essential equipment and guidance for the task of setting the newly rebuilt console into place. Piscitello furnished an aluminum beam capable of handling the weight of the console, the winches needed to hoist the console, and the trolley to roll the console over the choir railing and so it could be lowered into place. This equipment and Piscitello's supervision enabled the workers to hoist the larger chests into the choir loft, mitigating the back-breaking ordeal of carrying them up a lengthy flight of stairs and around a hairpin turn.

Anthony Piscitello, climbing the scaffolding. Bob Bunn and Ted Buck steadying the thousand-pound console while BHS student Craig Jarrett slowly pulls the console up into the choir loft. BHS student Rob Gonzales looking on and prepared to help. (Photo courtesy of Marlene Buck)

Bellevue High School athletes worked diligently Monday and Tuesday of Holy Week carrying out all assigned tasks cheerfully and diligently. They brought a breath of fresh air to the project along with the needed muscle to speed the installation along.

With all this carrying, heavy lifting, stacking, constructing the frame on which the organ would sit, etc., the need for sustenance for the volunteers and Bunn Minnick employees had not been overlooked by the women of the church. All during the installation process women of the church prepared lunches and dinners. There were two great advantages: First, the food was excellent! Second, the workers ate on site thus avoiding excessive down-time.

St. John's Fellowship Hall was "packed" with pipes and other organ parts during the return of the organ. But enough room was spared for serving food to the many workers and places for them to sit down and enjoy the delicious and abundant food prepared by the ladies of the church. (Photo courtesy of Marlene Buck)

The following is a list of congregational members and community volunteers who helped remove and/or re-install the organ, cook, and serve food to the workers, using their time and talents to bring this organ project to a successful conclusion:

Elizabeth Birr	Earl Koch	Alvin Mason	Betty Wahlers
Leonard Bowers	Georgine Koch	Clarice Mason	Glenn Wahlers
Marlene Buck	Bud Kryling	Edward Moyer	David Wietelmann
Theodore Buck	Jan LaBonte	Phyllis Neill	Jean Wietelmann
Dorothy Dick	Skip LaBonte	Anthony Piscitello	Charlotte Zimmerman
Ellen Dubbert	Karen Lieber	Donald Reiderman	Greg Zimmerman
Robert Dubbert	Paul Lieber	Dennis Rospert	
Jean Keiner	Brenda Manasco	Thomas Ruppert	
Delmar Koch	Gary Manasco	Alice Stoldt	

On Thursday, April 6, 1998, *The Bellevue Gazette* ran a front-page story by Jason Manner, Gazette staff writer, titled "Organ Transplant Nearly Complete'" with photos announcing the return of the organ to St. John's Lutheran Church.

"No church anywhere in the world is complete without the resounding sounds of a full pipe organ, for without the bellowing tones of celebration and exultation reverberating around the vaulted ceilings and the melodious combination of human and instrumental voices, a church is simply a place for prayer and worship.

For the St. John's Lutheran Church congregation on Southwest Street and the entire Bellevue community, the 10-month restoration and updating of the entire instrument was finally realized this week as it returned in boxes and pieces to its home. And what a better occasion to welcome her back than Easter Sunday.

With the help of many volunteers and the experts at Bunn Minnick Pipe Organs in Columbus this week, the countless boxes of pipes, cumbersome chests --- some weighing as much as 700 pounds --- and finally the console was either carried or carted into the church on Monday and Tuesday.

Once inside, a network of scaffolding, winches and plain old human ingenuity were used to hoist the chests and the console up to the choir loft. Once everything was there, the scaffolding had to be adjusted to get the larger chests up to their final resting place on the third level.

All told, over 2600 pipes or four divisions will be installed and tuned in the coming days and in time for Easter --- a painstaking process where each pipe must be tuned individually.

Unfortunately, the final piece of the instrument --- the Grand (sic) Division of 768 Pipes --- will not be installed in time for Easter Sunday as it is still being restored in Columbus...

"This project did not come together by chance. There was a lot of teamwork and volunteers to bring this to fruition. We are very pleased with the result and the congregation is very excited," Lieber pointed out..."

Because of Maundy Thursday and Good Friday services in St. John's Sanctuary, Bunn Minnick had to suspend work on the organ during those time frames. Friday night, all day and all-night Saturday, the Bunn Minnick crew worked feverishly to complete the Swell, Choir, and Solo divisions for the Sunrise Easter Service at 6:30 a.m. Working in shifts, some catching some sleep in the pews or in the lounge while the others worked, they finally finished the final tuning of the organ around 6 :10 a.m.

Our organist, Marlene Buck, not having any practice time on the organ, and was therefore unfamiliar with it, so Phil Minnick stayed during the Easter Sunrise Service to help Marlene. Phil set some pistons for the hymns and liturgy, pulled stops during the service, noted what manuals to use during her prelude, liturgy, postlude, etc.

With the Great division still absent from the organ, an immense amount of work had taken place and the time to thank those who had a part in this project was upon us. One group of individuals that played a critical part in our organ project were the students and athletes of Bellevue High School. On April 24, 1998, I wrote Dr. James Lahoski, Superintendent Bellevue City Schools, a letter naming these volunteer students and outlining the work they accomplished (copy of letter in possession of the author):

> "I take great pride in bringing to your attention a group of Bellevue High School students who over a period of ten months (June 1997-April 1998) volunteered their services for our pipe organ renovation project at St. John's Lutheran Church, Bellevue, Ohio."

Brad Clark	Adam Fries	Jonathan Manasco	Kit Ruffing
Jason Cochey	Nate Goebbel	Chris Miller	Brad Rohrbacher
Anthony Coleman	Robert Gonzales	Scott Miller	Philip Shumway
Matt De Polo	Jason Haugha-wout	Jeremy Pifer	Mark Slosser
Richard Felske	Craig Jarrett	Kirk Piscitello	Laramie Spurlock
Duke Fox	Peter Lepley	David Polley	

I went on to list the work and activities they had been involved in for the benefit of the organ project. Closing the letter, "Their integrity and hard work reflect the finest traditions of Bellevue High School and the community. With a deep sense of appreciation for a job well done, the organ committee, church council, congregation, and clergy of St. John's Lutheran Church wish to commend these twenty-three young men for their willingness to help our organ project."

*A listing of The Bunn Minnick Pipe Organ Company employees and associates who worked on this project can be found on page 98.

It was not until late May 1998 that the Great division of the organ was installed, just in time for Memorial Day weekend. The following ranks were put in place: 16' Gemshorn, 8' Prinzipal, 8' Holz Gedeckt, 4' Oktav, 2 2/3' Quinte, 2' Klein Oktav, III Mixtur, II Zymbel, and 8' Trompette Héroique. The organ was finally a complete instrument of 52 ranks.

The Organ Dedication Services took place on September 27, 1998

Organ Prelude   Prelude on "Engelberg"   James Pethel
           (When in Our Music God Is Glorified)
The Sounding of the Organ: Principals, Flutes, Strings, and Reeds
Opening Hymn: "A Mighty Fortress Is Our God"   *Ein Feste Burg*
A Hymn of Praise: "When in Our Music God Is Glorified"   *Engelberg*
Prayer of Day
Litany of Dedication
Choir Anthem: "I Will Extol Thee, My God, O King"   Henry Kihlken
    [The Choir commissioned Mr. Henry Kihlken to compose this anthem for our organ dedication service]
Children's Message:
Lessons and Psalm: I Samuel 1: 21-28a, Psalm 150, Revelation 4: 1-8
Contemporary Group Anthem:
Gospel Lesson: John 21: 15-19
Sermon:
Hymn: "The Church's One Foundation"   *Aurelia*
Creed:
Bell Choir Anthem:
Choir Anthem: "Worship God With Music"   Natalie Sleeth
Prayers and Blessing:
Closing Hymn: "Let All Things Now Living"   *The Ash Grove*
Postlude: "Grand Choeur"   Theodore Dubois

Participants:

    Pastor: The Reverend David Wietelmann
    Organist: Marlene Buck   Choir Director: Jan LaBonte
    Bell Choir Director: Robert Dubbert   Lay Reader: Paul Lieber
    Contemporary Group: Chris Young, Evelyn Woodruff, and Cindy Mira

The Tuesday, September 22, 1998, *Bellevue Gazette* ran a frontpage article announcing the dedication recital of the newly renovated and expanded organ.

"In celebration of its completion, Bellevue native and gifted organist, The Reverend Frank Stoldt, now living in Minnesota, will give a special recital on the organ on Sunday, September 27, at 3:30 p.m.

Stoldt, who grew up in the church and community, is the son of William and Alice Stoldt, Friedley Avenue. Frank is an accomplished and gifted organist. He currently serves as the director of Worship and Music for Augsburg Fortress, the publishing house for the Evangelical Lutheran Church in America."

Being a "son-of-the-parish," it was logical that he was chosen to play the inaugural recital on the St. John's organ, especially since he was introduced to the study of music (piano) by our parish organist, Marlene Buck. The recital program gave a short biography:

"He is a graduate of Bellevue High School, Heidelberg College, The Eastman School of Music, The Lutheran School of Theology at Chicago, and is currently a Ph.D. candidate at the Catholic University of America. His organ teachers included Grace Morris, Catherine Thiedt, David Craighead, and Peter Marshall. He has also studied improvisation with Gerre Hancock and Paul Mantz…"

The Organ Dedication Recital, September 27, 1998, The Reverend Frank Stoldt, Organist

God The Father:

Piece d' Orgue	J.S. Bach (1685-1750)
Hymn- *"Let All Things Now Living" LBW 557*	
Adagio in Sol minore	Tomaso Alblinoni (1671-1750)
Hymn- *"All Creatures of Our God and King" LBW 527* (Stanzas 1, 2, 3, 7 only)	

God The Son:

Two Preludes on "Ein Feste Burg"	Max Reger (1873-1916)
[LBW 228]	Dieterich Buxtehude (1637-1707)
Variations on "Westminster Abbey"	Richard Proulx (b. 1937)
Hymn- *"Jesus the Very Thought of You" LBW 316*	
Gospel Prelude on "What a Friend We Have in Jesus"	William Bolcom (b. 1938)
[LBW 439]	

God The Holy Spirit:

Prelude and Fugue in E Flat	J.S.Bach (1685-1750)
Song of Peace	Jean Langlais (1907-1991)
Hymn- *"Let Us Talents and Tongues Employ" WOV 754*	
Carillon de Westminster	Louis Vierne (1870-1937)

(Dedication <u>Recital Attendance 387</u>)

Twenty Years of Services, Concerts, and Silent Films 1998-2018:

With the afterglow of satisfaction for a job well done and the dedication recital still ringing in our ears, it was time to move forward with the use of the instrument. There was absolutely no doubt that the primary function of the organ was to provide music for our church services, special services, choir accompaniment, weddings, and funerals. Still, there was a great deal of down time in which the organ was not used. Bunn Minnick had built a large and versatile organ for St. John's, although it would be another twenty years before it reached its full tonal splendor.

A few weeks after the dedication recital, St. John's held an open house for the local organists to come and see the instrument up close and, if they wished, to play. I gave a short talk on the background of the organ. Marlene Buck played, noting the different ranks, and demonstrated how the computerization of the organ made it easier to play and the different levels of memory allowed for guest organists to set their own pistons. Charlotte Zimmerman and several ladies of the church had homemade cookies and coffee for the local organists after the presentation. In attendance were, Carol Schubert, Louise Swartz, Martha Cook, and Richard Dundore.

Although a great asset to St. John's music program, it seemed we should share this resource with the community at large. I approached the then Bellevue High School Director of Bands, Mr. Wayne McCoy, with a novel idea of having a concert at St. John's using the organ and the high school wind ensemble. I argued that such a concert would showcase both the wind ensemble and the organ in a form that was unusual for both. It would have the added advantage of congregational members, band parents, and community members in attendance for the concert in a venue that could seat a great many people.

After my initial approach to McCoy, we discussed some of issues a concert of this type would face. First, getting music for both the organ and wind ensemble to play together. Second, the set up for such an undertaking would be daunting: The pews in the choir loft would have to be removed, chairs and music stands for the wind ensemble brought in, transporting chairs, music stands, and all the musical instruments to the church, moving the 1,000-pound console from the middle of the choir loft off to the far south side. Third, setting a date that was amenable to both the school system and the church. Fourth, getting St. John's organist, Marlene Buck on board with the projected concert. And finally, getting permission from the congregational council and the Superintendent of Bellevue City Schools to have the concert.

After initial discussions with Marlene Buck, she came on board with the project almost immediately. Pastor Wietelmann supported the proposed concert, and the church council gave its approval. Dr. James Lahoski, Superintendent of Bellevue City Schools, after discussions with McCoy and me, supported the concert as well. Sunday, May 16, 1999, at 7:00 p.m. was the date and time chosen for this landmark Bellevue concert.

I took charge of the logistics, working along with McCoy and Marlene Buck to make this first organ/wind ensemble concert memorable, a success, and possibly the start of a series of organ/wind ensemble concerts. McCoy, Marlene Buck, and I discussed the music to be used. I had attended several "Concert of American Music" for the Fourth of July celebration at The National Cathedral (The Cathedral of Saint Peter and Saint Paul) in Washington, D.C. and recommended opening the concert with The Star-Spangled Banner, verse 1 and 4, as they did at The National Cathedral concerts, using both the organ and the wind ensemble. It made sense to open with the National Anthem because of the proximity of the concert to Memorial Day.

Once again, I turned to Bellevue High School athletes to provide the needed "muscle" to make the concert a success. Approaching head football coach, Ed Nasonti, he encouraged his players to be supportive of and aid in the preparations for this community concert. The athletes moved chairs and music stands to the church and helped set them up. But first, they had to remove all the heavy wooden pews from the choir loft and then move the 1,000-pound organ console to the south side of the choir loft without damaging it. They accomplished all the assigned tasks safely and expeditiously.

Artwork for the programs for this first organ/wind ensemble concert was given to a member of the art class, Joshua Zimmerman, grandson of the former financial chair of the organ committee, Milton Zimmerman. The Bellevue Board of Education supplied the paper and printed the programs.

A special guest travelled a great distance to hear this concert. Mrs. Lillian Reynolds was the first person the author encountered when I travelled to the Bunn Minnick facility to discuss St. John's pipe organ. She had been Bunn Minnick's office manager for 20 years. Lillian had retired and moved to Tucson, Arizona. We were delighted that she chose to fly back to Ohio to attend this concert!

Ms. Linda Hill would be a guest organist at this concert.

It was an exceptionally warm evening for the 7:00 p.m. concert. The heat caused the temperature in the pipe chamber to soar to a blistering 94 degrees. This forced McCoy to tune each of the individual instruments sharp to be in tune with the organ before the concert started.

"Pictured from left are Pam Hill, Josie Widman, Jason Ianello, Phil Shumway and Adrienne Felder, members of the Bellevue High School Wind Ensemble as they pose around the four manual (keyboard) console of the 52-rank pipe organ at St. John's Lutheran Church. The wind ensemble and organ will perform a concert at the church on Sunday, May 16 at 7p.m. (Gazette photo courtesy of Woodard Photographic Studio)" Front page of the Tuesday, May 11, 1999, issue of The Bellevue Gazette.

The Bellevue Wind Ensemble, Mr. Wayne A. McCoy, Director
Mr. David W. Strayer, Assistant Director
Mrs. Marlene Buck, Organist, St. John's Lutheran Church
Ms. Linda M. Hill, Organist, Peace Lutheran Church, Dayton, OH

The National Anthem, verses 1 & 4	Francis Scott Key
(Wind Ensemble & Marlene Buck, organ)	
Festival Prelude:	James Swearingen
(Wind Ensemble & Marlene Buck, organ)	
Joyful, Joyful	Ludwig van Beethoven
(Linda Hill, organ)	arr. Diane Bish
Die Meistersinger	Richard Wagner
(Wind Ensemble)	arr. Gene Milford
Old One Hundreth	Vaughn Williams
(Wind Ensemble & Marlene Buck, organ)	arr. Robert Washburn
Prelude on 'Londonderry Aire'	arr. Noel Rawsthorne
(Wind Ensemble)	
Finale from 'How Firm a Foundation'	arr. Janet Linker
(Linda Hill, organ)	
Finlandia	Jean Sibelius
(Wind Ensemble)	arr. Lucien Cailliet
America the Beautiful	Samuel A. Ward
(Wind Ensemble & Marlene Buck, organ)	arr. Carmen-Dragon
Hymn "America the Beautiful" (all stand and sing)	Samuel A. Ward (Music)
(Wind Ensemble & Marlene Buck, organ)	Katherine L. Bates (Text)

The organ wind ensemble concert lasted 50 minutes and ended with the 432 people in attendance, giving the musicians a thunderous standing ovation. This concert was a massive success, period! It brought together a large and versatile pipe organ, two organists capable of using it, a high school band director who wasn't afraid to try a novel new concert idea for his students, and the Bellevue High School Wind Ensemble musicians who were capable of performing at a high level in front of a large audience in a venue that was not typical of high school band concerts, and with an instrument that most of them had never performed with (see pages 99-101 for a complete listing of the wind ensemble musicians). Since the first organ/wind ensemble concert was such a rousing success, there would be two more planned one in 2001 and the last one in 2003.

Response from some of the attendees:

Cynthia Franks- "WOW!!!!! That was so good. I am so glad that Paul took the time to remind us all about it [Bellevue City Schools Faculty email]. The organ was spine-tingling. The wind ensemble was outstanding, amazingly, wonderfully beautiful..."

Ellen Blum- "Great Concert Sunday!"

Evelyn Woodruff- "I wanted to tell you how wonderful I thought it was. Everyone was truly moved at the magnificent sound. Thanks so much for organizing and overseeing the concert..."

Julie Cloud- "It was absolutely breathtaking. I was very proud Kevin was able to be part of it." (Mother of Kevin Cloud, Trombone)

Of special note was a thank you card sent to The Reverend David Wietelmann by Mrs. Elmer Diehr (Mrs. Diehr was a German national during the Nazi era in Germany and suffered at the hands of the Nazis. She married Elmer Diehr, an American soldier from Bellevue, moved to the United States and became a citizen).

"Dear Reverend Wietelmann, It was a real joy to attend last Sunday's concert. I had not heard such wonderful and moving presentation in a small town like ours. It was uplifting and just what I needed. Too bad many of my friends were not there to hear it...Thank you very much to you and all the people who made it possible. I grew up with classical music in Europe and never lost my love and appreciation for it."

Sally Boyd, *The Bellevue Gazette* Neighbors Editor, attended the concert after a long day of covering various end of year school events. Boyd's article, *The Bellevue Gazette*, Friday, May 21, 1998, is worth quoting at length:

"...Nearly two hours later, it was on to the final stop of the evening --- the 'Pomp and Pipes' concert by the BSHS Wind Ensemble teamed with gifted organists Marlene Buck and Linda Hill, who were to play the magnificent, restored pipe organ at St. John's Lutheran Church.
I have to admit, I was thinking very longingly of home, my recliner and the beginning segment of 'Joan of Arc'. Tempting as that was, I made what turned out to be the very best choice and a perfect way to cap off a good day. I went to the concert. If there was any doubt that Bellevue is amazingly blessed with gifted musical artisans, last Sunday's impressive concert should have instantly quieted any doubters. It was a stellar performance.
The student musicians are absolutely wonderful. Under the expert directorship of Wayne McCoy, who has challenged them to perform music often considered difficult even for experienced musicians, the Wind Ensemble truly rose to the occasion. Their music soared to the
heavens, a fitting delivery considering the church setting.
When teamed with the incredible 52 rank pipe organ that fills the upper reaches of the church sanctuary, I found my spirit soaring as well. It was clear by the crowd's reaction I was not alone.
Because the musicians were above and behind the audience, it was easy to focus on the music, rather than watching the musicians or the director. It was just us and the music --- truly an uplifting experience.
The music performed by the band/organ combination was enthralling. I found myself wondering if nearby residents and passersby were pausing to take in the glorious sound. They certainly could have and should have. There was no doubt the music was reaching far beyond the boundaries of walls and stained-glass windows.
Nearly 450 people --- again many from the day's previous two functions --- filled St. John's. The band/organ combination was so unique that the Bunn Minnick Co., which restored the organ, sent a contingent to record the concert and to hear how their restored instrument sounded when paired with a really good (superior even) high school band. They had to have been pleased.
Linda Hill, at 26, is a most gifted artist. Marlene Buck is St. John's equally talented organist. Both exhibited a delicacy of touch, contrasted with the incredible strength as they elicited a range of sound from the grand old organ that had to be heard to be believed.

From the opening of 'The National Anthem', through an exquisite rendition of Prelude on 'Londonderry Aire' and 'Finale' from 'How Firm a Foundation' to the most challenging 'Finlandia' and finally, the closing notes of 'America the Beautiful' with organ accompaniment arranged by Ms. Hill specifically for the concert, the audience was enthralled. Young, and old, tired or not, it was an experience that obviously brought great pleasure to many, many people and sent the spirit winging.

In the works for two years, the concert was the result of efforts by BSHS instructor (and St. John's member) Paul Lieber and Marlene Buck. It was through the organ restoration that they met Hill, organist for Peace Lutheran Church, in Dayton.

It took lots and lots of work by lots of people, not the least of whom were the BSHS Wind Ensemble, performing beautifully under the baton of Wayne McCoy.

Lieber, who served as commentator, noted the band's performance of 'Die Meistersinger' had also earned them a 'superior' rating during their recent state competition. In that contest, the kicker (which caused no small amount of concern) was that the band's adjudicator was also the man who actually arranged the required piece. He, too, awarded them a superior. Quite a feat from one who, no doubt, was a tough critic.

Lieber also credited the 'behind the scenes' effort by many BSHS students, including many who have no musical bent whatsoever. To fit the band into the organ/choir loft, students had to move the half-ton organ console to one side and take pews out. The whole process was reversed on Tuesday when all the pieces/parts were put back into their usual places.

Since Sunday, as the days and hours have dragged on and on, it's been difficult to imagine a more uplifting experience than Sunday's crowning concert. It was certainly one I was delighted to experience and one which, as enervation and fatigue settle in, I recapture over and over again in memory.

As I hear the music reverberate in my mind, my spirit again takes flight. This one event alone will keep me going for the remainder of the school year and I thank St. John's and the high school musicians for their gift."

In addition to the general praise the participants of the concert received, organist Marlene Buck felt immense satisfaction having played with several of her former kindergarten students who were members of the wind ensemble. After the concert ended several of her former students made their way to the organ to speak with her. "Mrs. Buck, you were great, and you shook the floor!" Later, Marlene told me the praise she received from her former students and being able to play with them meant more to her than anything else that evening.

With unbounded praise for the organ/wind ensemble from the media and members of the community that attended the concert, it was apparent that this would not be the last organ/wind ensemble concert. With the extra planning, organization, music to be learned, and re-configuring of the choir loft, it was decided that the concerts would take place on an every- other-year basis. There would be two more organ/wind ensemble concerts, one in 2001 and the last one in 2003.

The organ and church would take a hiatus from concerts until the next organ/wind ensemble concert in 2001. During this time, the church used the organ for its primary purpose, leading the music of the congregation on Sundays, festival celebrations such as Reformation, Christmas, Easter, Pentecost, and part of the Saturday night 5:00 p.m. services (The Saturday Night Service being a blend of contemporary and traditional music where the organ was also used along with guitars and a synthesizer).

Additional use of the organ for organ/wind ensemble concerts, "Young Organists Concerts", and Silent Films would start in 2001 and continue through 2013. Thus, St. John's investment of time, money, and effort paid extraordinary dividends well beyond its primary role of leading the church services for which it was originally intended.

As May of 2001 drew closer, planning and organizing for the May 20, 2001 organ/wind ensemble concert moved into high gear. Once again, the oak pews in the choir loft had to be removed and the organ console moved to the south side of the choir loft. As had been the case in 1999, Bellevue High School athletes lent a helping hand. The "many hands" were- Josh Hirt, Zach Huston, Sean Rowley, Justin Walters, Tommy Weakland, Joe Smith, and Quenton Smith.

Amy Bowers, congregational member, and daughter of Lennie and Kathy Bowers, with her French Horn, standing behind the Skinner 8' French Horn rank located in the Solo Division. (Photo by author)

Members of the 2001 Bellevue High School Wind Ensemble at the console of the organ. Front row Amy Bowers, and Emily Valko, back row Joel Wietelmann, Dave Reigel, Erik Knight, Bill King, and Doug Smith. (Photo by author)

The local media outlets were notified and ran articles or made announcements to "get the word out." On Wednesday, May 16, 2001, *The Bellevue Gazette* ran an article detailing the time and date, music to be heard, and some of the participants: "Utilizing two community assets, The Bellevue High School Wind Ensemble and St. John's 3,416 pipe organ, a concert of 60 to 65 minutes will be performed...Even in large cities organ/wind ensemble concerts are the exception..."

Not only would the 2001 organ/wind ensemble concert have new music, some newer members of the wind ensemble, but it would also include a "Patriotic Sing Along" as the final part of the concert.

Pomp & Pipes
Music for Organ and Wind Ensemble
Sunday, May 20, 2001, at 7:00 PM
The Bellevue Wind Ensemble, Director Wayne A. McCoy
David W. Strayer, Assistant Director
Mrs. Marlene S. Buck, Organist St. John's Lutheran Church

The National Anthem, verse 1 & 4	Francis Scott Key
(Wind Ensemble & Marlene Buck, organ)	
Fanfare Prelude	arr. James Swearingen
(Wind Ensemble, Marlene Buck, organ)	
Tuba Tune in D Major	C.S. Lang
(Marlene Buck, organ)	
From Whom All Blessings Flow	arr. Ed Huckeby
(Wind Ensemble)	
Holy, Holy, Holy	John B. Dykes
(Wind Ensemble & Marlene Buck, organ)	arr. Wayne Stevens
"Paraphrase" Sur un Chœur de Judas Macchabée	Alexandre Guilmant
De Händel (Marlene Buck, organ)	
Prelude on An Old English Hymn	arr. Robert Sheldon
(Wind Ensemble)	
America the Beautiful	Samuel A. Ward
(Wind Ensemble & Marlene Buck, organ)	arr. Carmen-Dragon
Patriotic Hymn Sing (Marlene Buck, organ)	

"Eternal Father Strong to Save" (Navy Hymn)

"America the Beautiful"

"God of Our Fathers" (addition of wind ensemble brass)

"My Country Tis of Thee"

"The Battle Hymn of the Republic" (addition of wind ensemble, refrain)

"God Bless America"

Just prior to the "Patriotic Hymn Sing" Mrs. Buck surprised the audience and wind ensemble members with an encore. Marlene had been looking for a piece that would be fun to play and catch everyone's ear. On a trip to Columbus, Ohio to search for music at University Music, Marlene explained to well-known Columbus organist, Dorothy Riley, what she wanted. Ms. Riley immediately pulled out a piece and said, "Here Marlene, take this one!" *Hornpipe Humoresque: A Nautical Extravaganza for Organ*, by Noel Rawsthorne (1929-2019).

If you are familiar with the theme to "Popeye the Sailor Man", then this piece is for you! The composition is a set of amusing variations in the styles of various composers (with apologies to the composers): J.S. Bach, Vivaldi, Arne, and Widor.

Young and old alike immediately recognized the theme and chuckled throughout the entire piece. The ovation from all in attendance was immediate and powerful.

"The Patriotic Hymn Sing", one verse of every song, capped an already successful concert. All in attendance sang their hearts out. By the time Mrs. Buck rolled into *God Bless America* the singing had reached thunderous proportions and almost overpowered the organ until she went to Tutti on the last chord.

Attendance at this the second in the series of Organ/Wind Ensemble Concert rose to 468. And the praise rolled in: The Ocker Family, "Mr. Lieber, Thanks for the wonderful entertainment last night…I wanted to be part of the crowd, and I was not sorry. Congratulations to your church and to the students as well. God bless all…" Clarice Mason, "Paul, Thanks for setting up the concert last Sunday. What a Joy it is to hear the beautiful music and to know that Bellevue has such great musicians coming from our music program…" Dorothy Pickering, a local organist, harpist, and composer, "Great concert last night! It's always so exciting to hear that organ join in with the band…Hope St. John's does that again next year…Good job by all."

In the Thursday, May 24, 2001, edition of The Bellevue Gazette, Karen Chapman wrote a letter to the editor under the title "Enjoyed Organ Concert":

"To the editor:
Bellevue was presented an excellent concert Sunday evening, May 20, by Marlene Buck and the Bellevue High School Wind Ensemble under the direction of Wayne Mccoy. I am sure the applause could not have fully expressing (sic) the feelings and appreciation the audience was experiencing.

The selections touched a person's spirit, allowed a sing-along to voice a person's pride in our country and our freedom, and even a light-hearted selection, presented by Mrs. Buck, that showed a little of the pipe organ's versability.

To Marlene Buck and to each member of the Wind Ensemble, thank you very much for an excellent concert. It was truly enjoyed.

A thank you to Wayne McCoy, director of the Wind Ensemble, and David Strayer, assistant director, for their dedication to an instrumental program that not only expands their student's abilities and experiences but allows the people of Bellevue to enjoy their student's musical accomplishments.

A thank you to Paul Lieber, chairman of the Organ Committee of St. John's Lutheran Church, for acting as host for the evening, and I am sure a lot of behind-the-scenes work.

To those involved through the St. John's Lutheran Church, thank you for your openness in presenting this excellent concert in your facility at no cost to those attending.

It is unknown to me who began the inspiration for such a concert but once started it takes commitment and organization from many people --- a big thank you goes out to everyone connected."

Continuing into the church service on Saturday, May 26, 2001, some of the young musicians and choir members of Bellevue High School were far from finished with providing the congregation of St. John's and the community with uplifting music. This time it would be at the 5:00 p.m. Saturday Night Service at St. John's.

At this service, BHS Freshman Quenton Smith and I would handle the use of the organ. A brass and percussion ensemble composed of BHS students: On trumpet Joel Wietelmann, Erik Knight, and Tim Gerhardstein, and Doug Smith percussion and piano. Ms. Carrie Criswell, Choral Music Instructor at Bellevue High School, and 25 members of her choir added their voices and enhanced the service.

Music For the Saturday May 26, 2001, Service

Prelude (Paul Lieber, organ)	"Theme on Morganlied"
Hymn (Quenton Smith, organ; brass and percussion)	"God of Our Fathers"
Hymn of the Day (Quenton Smith, organ)	"Let All Things Now Living"
Offertory (Doug Smith, piano)	
Hymn (Quenton Smith, organ; Doug Smith, piano; and trumpets)	"How Great Thou Art"
Hymn (Quenton Smith, organ; Doug Smith percussion; and trumpets)	"Onward Christian Soldiers"
Choral Benediction (BHS Choir members)	
Postlude (Paul Lieber, organ)	

For almost a year, the organ returned exclusively to its primary role of leading the church services from Reformation through, Advent, Christmas, Epiphany, Lent, Holy Week and Easter. But the end of April brought a "new" type of concert to St. John's Lutheran Church.

On Sunday evening, April 28, 2002, St. John's sponsored a concert called "An Organ Spectacular" with J. Clark Wilson at the console. Clark Wilson was no stranger to St. John's or to our organ. Bunn Minnick had Wilson voice the 16' Tuba rank, the Skinner 8' French Horn, and later in 2003 the Skinner 8' English Horn that would complete our Solo Division. Clark spent several years at The Schantz Organ Company as a reed voicer and tonal finisher.

Clark's professional career began with his appointment as the featured organist post at Pipe Organ Pizza in Milwaukee, Wisconsin. Wilson performed at numerous regional and national conventions for The American Theater Society and gave a series of highly lauded workshops for Young People's Pipe Organ Encounters. Wilson has performed concerts in the United States, Canada, Great Britain, and Australia. He has done extensive silent film accompaniment, including at The Chautauqua Institution in New York, at the University of California at Los Angeles (UCLA), and for the Academy of Arts and Sciences in Los Angeles. He is the featured organist for the Summer Movie Series at the famed Ohio Theater in Columbus, Ohio, and was chosen by the Columbus Association Performing Arts (CAPA) to re-premier the renowned Chicago Theater Wurlitzer organ. Wilson is the only individual to receive both The Technician of the Year Award (1993) and Organist of the Year Award (1998) from The American Theater Organ Society (ATOS). At the time of this concert, Clark was a professor at the University of Oklahoma teaching silent film accompaniment and composition, the first such organ course in The United States since the late 1920s.

Wilson has given all-transcription recitals for the American Guild of Organists and played for The Organ Historical Society. He would do the same at St. John's Lutheran Church on the evening of April 28, 2002. Quoting from the program:

"This evening we will hear a different kind of organ music, music that was popular eighty years ago at organ recitals, when huge municipal organs dotted the country and were the vehicle for bringing orchestral works to the people. Tonight's program includes a few works written for organ, some lighter numbers that might have been heard on "reproducing" player pipe organs in the home of the wealthy, but mostly transcribed works from the masters as brought to the organ.

Most of these have long since become standard "warhorse" pieces beloved of generations: we hope you will also enjoy them as dressed in the incomparable colors of the pipe organ."

On a cold, rainy, late April, Sunday night, Clark Wilson lit up the church with a spectacular concert, the likes of which St. John's and Bellevue had never heard before.

PART I

Prelude To Act III-Lohengrin (Wagner)
To a Wild Rose (MacDowell)
Trumpet Tune (Johnson)
Serenade (Pierne)
Dawn (Jenkins)
War March of the Priests (Mendelsohn)

Part II

Pomp and Circumstance #4 (Elgar)
Fountain Reverie (Fletcher)
Entry of the Toreadors-Carmen (Bizet)
Pastorale on Forest Green (Purvis)
Finlandia (Sibelius)
Encore: *Nobles of the Mystic Shrine* (Sousa)

The ovation at the end of the concert lifted the roof. To the delight of the audience Wilson had pulled almost every conceivable color out of the 52-rank organ: Sweet, pensive, contemplating, march-like, joyous, and thunderous! At the end of the concert Wilson, always the gracious musician, spent time with the young people who were practicing, providing special music, playing services, or just plain interested in the organ at St. John's. It is rare that young musicians, young organists, and simply interested parties, can have conversations with accomplished professional musicians of Clark Wilson's caliber, let along unrushed, take your time, discussions, and "let's go up to the organ and I'll show you." This would not be the last time Wilson would "wow" the audiences at St. John's Lutheran Church.

It would not be long before these young organists and musicians would utilize what Clark Wilson had discussed and showed them on the organ after the April 2002 concert.

Hmmm, so that's what a 16' Tuba looks like! Standing in the Solo Division of the organ at St. John's are left to right Joe Smith, Quenton Smith, and Erik Knight. These three Bellevue High School student/athletes will share their musical talents on the organ at the 5:00 p.m., Saturday, May 25, service where they were joined by a brass choir of fellow BHS students and a choral community choir. The metal pipes in the background are part of the 16' Quintadena. (Photo by author)

The music for this service was a blend of Trinity Sunday and Memorial Day. The three pictured organists were joined by Paul Lieber on organ, and a brass choir under the direction of Wayne A. McCoy, BHS Director of Bands. The Brass choir members were David Strayer (Assistant Band Director), Jake Knight, Eric Daniel, David Wallingford, Christa Schultz, Joel Wietelmann, Randy Yates, Aaron Ammanniti, Diana Hackenburg, and Emily Foisy; playing trumpets, trombones, tubas, French Horns, and percussion.

Special guest soloist, Jake Knight of the Miami University Jazz Band played duets with his brother Erik, and Quenton Smith.

A community choir, under the direction of Mrs. Lynn McCoy and accompanied by Erik Knight on the organ, sang Peter J. Wilhousky's arrangement of *The Battle Hymn of the Republic* during the offertory and added their impressive voices to the service hymns and "The Patriotic Sing Along."

Order of Service (Musical)

Prelude:	*Holy, Holy, Holy*	Quenton Smith, organ & Brass Choir
Opening Hymn:	*Holy, Holy, Holy*	Quenton Smith, organ & Brass Choir
Hymn of Day:	*Eternal Father Strong to Save*	Erik Knight, organ & Brass Choir
Offertory:	*Battle Hymn of the Republic*	Erik Knight, organ & Community Choir
Communion:	*Beneath the Cross of Jesus*	Quenton Smith, organ
	Precious Lord Take My Hand	Erik Knight, organ & Jake Knight, Sax
Closing Hymn:	*Onward Christian Soldiers*	Quenton Smith, organ & Brass Choir

At the end of the service instead of the traditional Postlude, a "Patriotic Sing Along" took place.

America the Beautiful	Joe Smith, organ & Brass Choir (one verse)
Battle Hymn of the Republic	Erik Knight, organ & Brass Choir (two verses; plus, brass 2nd verse)
The National Anthem	Paul Lieber, organ & Brass Choir

The applause at the end of the service for all these young musicians was prolonged from the grateful worshipers. It gave all the participants in the service a great sense of pride and satisfaction. The community choir and Erik Knight did an outstanding job on *The Battle Hymn of the Republic*, while at the same time, the choir added immensely to the singing of hymns during and after the service. It was a positive and uplifting service for the guests and congregational people and the participants as well.

The Trinity/Memorial Day service went over so well that it was decided we would try it again at the Saturday service, December 21, 2002. This time these talented musicians would help bring in the Christmas season. Erik Knight and Quenton Smith would be the organists. A brass choir of Bellevue High School students included: David Wallingford, tuba; Diana Hackenberg and Amy Bowers, French Horn; Andrew Bishop and Aaron Ammanniti, trombone; Nick Linkenhoker, Erin Bowns, Brandon Good, Mike Snyder, and Christa Schultz, trumpets; Grace Fry, percussion.

The Wednesday, December 18, 2002, edition of *The Bellevue Gazette* ran a front-page article about the up-and-coming church service. Quoting from that article:

"…BSHS students Quenton Smith and Erik Knight, organists, will be accompanied by 14 brass and percussion players."

"Teenagers tend to get a bad rap," said Paul Lieber, who organized the service, "because the public sometimes concentrates on this age group's negative aspects. Here we have 16 teenage volunteers in God's house, honing their skills, to play for God's church services. This is a win-win situation for the teens, St. John's, and the Bellevue community."

"It is really an honor to play such a beautiful instrument," said Knight. "Rarely do you find an organ of this caliber in a small town. This is the third time I have played with a high school brass group and it's always been a fun, musically challenging experience."

"I particularly like to hear people sing along with us as we play. You have to concentrate when you play the organ, but hearing the brass play and voices sing along with you is awesome," add Smith.

Nick Linkenhoker commented, "I had really heard great things about the organ and this brass group, so when the opportunity arose to play with them, I jumped at it. I can hardly wait to hear the congregation sing along with us."

"I like to be involved in community service, but I particularly like playing with the organ and the brass group. The way the music all comes together is really neat," quipped Aaron Ammanniti. Lieber added it takes a great deal of practice and arranging of music for the service to Come together.

"Christa Schultz, a senior at BSHS, deserves special mention. I just hand the organ score to Christa and she goes home and transposes the music into the right key for the appropriate instrument."

Several musicians were impacted by the religious and ecumenical aspect of playing together. "It's really nice to be able to gather musicians of different faiths and play for both the congregation and God," noted Erin Bowns.

David Wallingford enjoys playing the tuba, "but for me, playing a hymn on an instrument is my way of worshipping God. I'm happy for the chance to play in this ensemble."

Andrew Bishop tied it all together. "I love music. To me music is a voice from the soul that brings people of different creeds, cultures, and religions together to worship in their own special way."

Seated going counterclockwise from the left David Wallingford, Diana Hackenburg, Amy Bowers, Andrew Bishop, Aaron Ammanniti, Nick Linkenhoker, Erin Bowns, Brandon Good, Mike Snyder, and Christa Schultz. Grace Fry, seated in the center, and organists Erik Knight and Quenton Smith stand by the console. Dane McCoy not pictured. (Gazette photo by Sally Boyd)

The enthusiasm of the brass choir members, as reflected in the *Gazette* article, was testament to their love of music, playing in a religious venue, and performing with the St. John's organ. The service was exceptionally well received by those in attendance and ended with the congregation joining the brass choir and the organ, in a booming rendition of *Joy to the World*.

As the time approached for the planning of the 2003 Organ/Wind Ensemble Concert in May, St. John's organist, Marlene Buck, informed the author that she would be unavailable to play the concert because of a family commitment on the same day as the concert, Sunday, May 18. Turning to Clark Wilson as a possible organist, Wilson instead recommended a young dynamic organist he knew, Brett Valliant. Clark made the first contact with Valliant to inquire if he would be interested in playing with the Bellevue High School Wind Ensemble and he answered in the affirmative.

Unlike St. John's in-house organist, Valliant, the organist at The First United Methodist Church in Wichita, Kansas, would require transportation to Bellevue and payment for his services. St. John's did not have this monetary hurdle for the previous two organ/wind ensemble concerts, so I (author) approached Mrs. Charlotte Zimmerman to see if she could help. Charlotte was one of the most gracious and giving individuals I have ever known. After explaining the monetary need for the securing Brett Valliant as our guest organist, she told the author that she would pay for the flight and Valliant's fee. Like most of Charlotte's generous giving to St. John's, she wanted her "contribution" to the success of the concert kept confidential which it was until now. Quoting from the concert program:

"Born in 1981 in Wichita, Kansas, Brett showed an interest in the organ at age three. Initially he played by ear and took piano lessons until he persuaded his parents to allow him to take up organ. By age eleven Brett played in church and continued his classical organ studies. He played his first classical organ concert at age fifteen. Although not thrilled with the idea at the time, Brett attended a concert featuring the Wichita Wurlitzer. He loved the theater organ and the rest, as they say, is history.

Turning down several prestigious classical organ positions, Brett has vigorously pursued his interest in theater organs. He toured Australia and New Zealand for five weeks, playing several organs in those two nations. Brett was elected president of the Wichita chapter of the American Theater Organ Society, has cut a CD called "Lyric Wurlitzer", and is the organist for The First United Methodist Church in Wichita."

The Friday, May 16, *The Bellevue Gazette* ran an article about the upcoming organ/wind ensemble concert, professional organist Brett Valliant, and the wind ensemble, *BSHS musicians join 'wunderkind' for concert at St. John's Lutheran,* ran the by-line, along with a photo of several wind ensemble members at the organ console.

"Fifty-eight members of the Bellevue High School Wind Ensemble will play a concert With St. John's Lutheran Church's organ on Sunday, May 18, at 4 p.m. Brett J. Valliant, from Wichita, Kan., will be the featured organist.

Brett Valliant is a sort of "wunderkind" when it comes to professional organists. He is Only 22 years old, stated Paul Lieber the concert coordinator. "But don't let his age fool you," continued Lieber, "he has played many of the largest organs in The United States, toured Australia and New Zealand playing concerts and has cut a CD already. He is an astonishing talent and very eager to play with some of Bellevue's finest musicians."

Erik Knight, first trumpet in the wind ensemble and an organist himself said, "It's always fun to accompany this organ with the Wind Ensemble or with a smaller brass choir. The applause at the last Organ/Wind Ensemble Concert gave me the chills. The audience was the loudest I have ever heard at any band concert I have played for."

Curt Hill, a saxophonist, interjected, "I am thrilled that a professional organist like Mr. Valliant will be making the trip all the way from Kansas to perform with us. I would encourage members of the community to attend this worthwhile performance."
This is the third organ/wind ensemble biannual concert.

"To our knowledge no other high school wind ensemble in north central Ohio plays a concert of this type," noted Lieber. "I think that is a tribute to the talent and dedication of our musicians, the vision and leadership provided by their director, Wayne McCoy, and the strong support for this concert series from both the administration of Bellevue City Schools and the church council of St. John's Lutheran Church…."

"Members of the Bellevue Senior High School Wind Ensemble take a moment to relax at the console of St. John's Lutheran Church's 3,477-pipe organ. Pictured from left are, Adrianna Ortiz, Erik Knight, Christa Schultz, Erin Bowns, Andrew Bishop, and Laura Huff. The BSHS Wind Ensemble will be performing a concert with the organ Sunday at 4 p.m." Photo provided by author to The Bellevue Gazette.

A second and unknown "hitch" had developed a few days before the Sunday concert. When I arrived at Cleveland Hopkins International Airport to pick up Valliant, unbeknownst to me, Valliant had just pulled himself out of a hospital bed that morning to make the flight to Ohio. Valliant had been struck down with a serious case of bronchitis. Recovering, but still "under the weather", Valliant put the best face on the situation and my wife Karen, and I made him as comfortable as possible in our home. To be frank, we didn't want to lose a second organist, this time to an illness! There would be almost no time left to find a replacement. Thankfully, Brett bounced back rapidly.

With St. John's organist at a family event, the church needed an organist or organists to play the May 18 8:00 a.m. and 10:30 a.m. services. Linda Thorbahn, a talented local organist, agreed to play the 8:00 a.m. service. This allowed Quenton Smith and Erik Knight, two of our high school organists, to play the 10:30 a.m. service. They would be joined by Brett Valliant, who would play the postlude.

The 10:30 a.m. Service opened with Erik Knight on the organ. Erik's prelude was Charles Marie Widor's *Toccata* the final movement from his *Fifth Organ Symphony*. A difficult piece to play for a professional organist, let along an eighteen-year-old high school senior. Quenton Smith, a high school junior, handled the hymns (*Let All Things Now Living, How Great Thou Art, and God of Our Fathers*), while Erik Knight took the liturgy and offertory. I had asked Brett Valliant to play a specific piece for the postlude and he graciously agreed. As the worshippers slowly left the Sanctuary, Valliant cut loose with the *Finale* to Charles Marie Widor's *Second Organ Symphony*. The worshippers exiting the Sanctuary slowed to a trickle as the booming strains of Widor's piece soared. One would have thought all the glass in the church would have been shattered with the thunderous ending to the *Finale*. Those in attendance at church had been given a taste to what was to come at the Organ/Wind Ensemble Concert later that afternoon.

Unfortunately, it turned out that this third organ/wind ensemble concert would be the final one of the series, but it would be attended by 517 people, by far the largest crowd to date. Being the last organ/wind ensemble by no means meant it was boring. In fact, the musicians brought the series to a triumphant end. A new wrinkle was brought to the fore. The organ would also be used with the Bellevue High School Jazz Band. A new twist that the audience, Jazz Band, and Brett Valliant found really entertaining.

Once again Bellevue High School student/athletes provided the "muscle" and where-with-all to empty the choir loft of pews and move the half ton organ console of the southern-most point in the choir loft. It took many hands and stout backs to make this concert a success: Jonathon Journay, Erik Knight, Matt Lepley, Ben Mallot, Kevin Riggleman, Joe Smith, Quenton Smith, Luke Spurlock, Jim Sturgill, and Jarrett Yingling.

Three students from the Bellevue High School Choir aided St. John's ushers in seating the attendees for the concert: Laurie Patrick, Karen Lepley, and Kasey Lepley.

Pomp and Pipes
Featuring Brett Valliant, Organist
The Bellevue High School Wind Ensemble and Jazz Band
Mr. Wayne A. McCoy, Director and Mr. David W. Strayer, Assistant Director
Music for Organ and Wind Ensemble
Sunday, May 18, 2003, at 4:00 PM

The National Anthem, verse 1 & 4	Francis Scott Key
(Wind Ensemble & Brett Valliant, organ)	
Danny Boy	ar. James Swearingen
(BHS Wind Ensemble)	
Toccata	John Weaver
(Brett Valliant, organ)	
Princeton Variations on "Holy, Holy, Holy"	David Schaffer
(BHS Wind Ensemble)	
Pomp and Circumstance No. 1	Sir Edward Elgar
(BHS Wind Ensemble & Brett Valliant, organ)	
Battle Hymn of the Republic	arr. Peter J. Wilhousky,
(Brett Valliant, organ)	transcribed for organ by
	Brett Valliant
America the Beautiful	Carmen-dragon
(BHS Wind Ensemble & Brett Valliant, organ)	
Lest We Forget	James Swearingen
(BHS Wind Ensemble)	

Intermission

Dancing Men	John LeBarera
(BHS Jazz Band & Brett Valliant, organ)	arr. Paul Lavender

70

The Girl From Ipanema   Antonio Jobim
(BHS Jazz Band & Brett Valliant, organ)   arr. Victor Lopez
Totem Pole   Frank Como and
(BHS Jazz Band & Brett Valliant organ)   Pat De Rosa

Stars and Stripes Forever   John Philip Sousa
(BHS Wind Ensemble & Brett Valliant, organ)
                    Patriotic Sing-Along (Brett Valliant, organ)
Eternal Father Strong to Save (2 verses)
God of Our Fathers (4 verses)
America the Beautiful (4 verses)

Thus ended, one of the most successful musical collaborations the City of Bellevue had ever enjoyed: our talented high school musicians and the pipe organ at St. John's Lutheran Church. The audience roared their approval with a long-standing ovation. Immediately following the concert, a reception for the musicians and the attendees was held in St. John's Fellowship Hall, refreshments being supplied by the ladies of the church.

Toward the end of the reception Brett Valliant and a group of enthusiastic followers went back to the organ: wind ensemble members, young organists who played at St. John's, Bunn Minnick employees, and people who just wanted to see how the organ was played. Valliant played several pieces and parts of various other compositions for the assembled group.

Brett Valliant at the console of St. John's organ. Valliant and the Bellevue High School Wind Ensemble played a spectacular concert. He is pictured here playing after the reception in the Fellowship Hall following the concert. Philip Minnick, President of the Bunn Minnick Pipe Organ Company, is in the background. (Photo by author)

Notes of appreciation rolled into the St. John's, Bellevue High School, and to the author.

"Dear Paul, just a note of thanks for the outstanding musical program at your church, Sunday. Wow!! The Wind Ensemble from the school sounded terrific as well as the very talented Brett Valliant.

To have such an outstanding organ and talented musicians from our hometown is remarkable. I know it must be a lot of hard work arranging everything, especially the timing Sunday with the honor awards at the school, too.

The selection of songs was so appropriate, and both Walter and I enjoyed every minute. Hope you will continue this another year. Many thanks, Eloise Horn"
(Letter in possession of author)

The Friday, May 23, 2003, edition of the Bellevue Gazette carried a short letter to the editor:

"To the Editor: We would like to express our appreciation and thanks to the Lutheran Church for hosting together with the Bellevue City School, the concert "Pomp and Pipes".
What a treat! Bellevue should be thankful and proud to have such talented young people, teachers, and artists.
I have not heard such a beautiful concert since I left Europe. The guest organist, Brett Valliant added a special sound. It was an excellent performance. Mr. & Mrs. Elmer Diehr"

Wayne McCoy, Director of Bellevue Bands, reminisced after the third and final concert about his and the Wind Ensemble's experiences during this concert series.

"In the Fall of 1998 you (the author) approached me about putting together an organ wind ensemble concert. I was a little apprehensive at first, but the more I thought about it, such a concert would be a perfect chance for community members unfamiliar with the high school wind ensemble's program, to hear just how impressive the student musicians really were.
Also, it was a chance to perform in a very unique venue for the wind ensemble and with a large pipe organ. To my knowledge, the pairing of a high school wind ensemble and a pipe organ had never been done in this part of Ohio.

Logistics presented a real challenge. First, all the pews in the choir loft had to be removed in order to fit the entire wind ensemble in the space. Room to accommodate the large percussion instruments had to be found. The organ console had to be moved off to one side of the choir loft to facilitate the high school musicians. On my part, I had to reconfigure the instrumentalists in the space available that would work for both the musicians and the organist. Last, but not least, the music stands, and chairs had to be trucked from the high school to the church, unloaded, and then set up.

I remember after the first rehearsal; the students were in awe at the tremendous sound the wind ensemble and organ made when performing together.

Wind ensemble parents, church and community members, and people from the surrounding area, were very receptive to all three concerts (1999, 2001, 2003). Attendance grew with each passing performance. At the 2003 concert we even used the Jazz Band with the organ, which elicited an enthusiastic response from the audience. It was a great experience for both myself and the student musicians to successfully perform such a unique and challenging concert. As I look back, I am proud to have been part of this singular set of performances and to have provided these rare experiences to my wind ensemble musicians. It was one of those memories that will live on forever for everyone that was involved."

With the final organ/wind ensemble concert a smashing success, plans were in the works for a young organists' concert to be held sometime late summer. Quenton Smith and Erik Knight both had a bird's-eye view of Brett Valliant during and after the concert. Smith was seated in the choir loft next to Valliant and Knight was first trumpet in the wind ensemble. Needless-to-say, they were awed by Valliant's ability on the instrument. But time was fast approaching when both

Smith and Knight would be playing their own organ concert with a brass choir composed mostly of classmates from Bellevue High School.

With the approval of St. John's congregational council, the first *Fireworks for Organ and Brass* was set for Sunday, August 17, 2003, at 7:00 p.m. A brass choir, under the direction of Mr. Wayne McCoy, would play a large part in the concert.

Trumpet	French Horn	Trombone	Tuba
Christa Schultz	Amy Bowers	Aaron Ammanniti	David Strayer
Mike Snyder	Diana Hackenburg	David Wallingford	Kim Knight
Nick Linkenhoker		Brian Hopkins	
Erin Bowens	Percussion		
Rachel Smith	Dan Pifer		
Chris Meadows	Dane McCoy		

Fireworks for Organ and Brass
Erik Knight and Quenton Smith, Organists
Brass Choir Under the Direction of
Mr. Wayne A. McCoy

The National Anthem, verse 1 & 4   Francis Scott Key
(Quenton Smith, organ & Brass Choir)
Fanfare For the Common Man   Aaron Copland
(Quenton Smith, organ; Dan Pifer, Timpani, Dane McCoy, Gong)
Prière à Notre Dame, from Suit Gothique   Leon Boëllmann
(Erik Knight, organ)
Song: Onward Christian Soldiers (all verse)   Arthur S. Sullivan
(Quenton Smith, organ & Brass Choir)
Fanfare   William Mathias
(Erik Knight, organ)
Song: God of Our Fathers (all verses)   George W. Warren
(Quenton Smith, organ and Brass Choir)
Olympic Fanfare   John Williams
(Erik Knight, organ)
Song: America the Beautiful (all verses)   Samuel A. Ward
(Erik Knight, organ & Brass Choir)   Katherine Lee Bates
Toccata, from the Fifth Organ Symphony   Charles Marie Widor
(Erik Knight, organ)
Song: High Hopes   James Van Heusen
(Erik Knight, organ…closed the concert on a light note)

Attendance at this mid-August concert was note-worthy. Four hundred and fifty-five people from the community and surrounding area came to hear the young organists and the brass choir on a warm August evening. The audience gave the organists, brass choir members, and Wayne McCoy a standing ovation. The ladies of St. John's had prepared a reception for all the musicians that had participated in the concert and their families. Homemade cookies and pastries were the fare of the evening.

Just prior to the *Fireworks for Organ and Brass Concert*, the last addition to the organ was purchased. In March 1998 when the Swell, Choir, and Solo divisions of the organ were re-installed, Bunn Minnick had prepared a chest in the Solo Division and the console for an 8'

English Horn rank. In early August 2003, St. John's agreed to purchase the Skinner Opus 466 English Horn. Charlotte Zimmerman funded the purchase of this rank at a cost of $3,200. The price included the purchase of the pipes, cleaning and repair, voicing, and on-site installation. The early Fall installation of the Skinner English Horn rank completed the organ as envisioned by Bunn Minnick.

Interest in playing St. John's pipe organ had been building among high school musicians. The success of the three Organ/Wind Ensemble Concerts, the use of young organists Erik Knight and Quenton Smith with brass choirs for church services, and the very successful first *Fireworks for Organ and Brass Concert* all contributed to the organ's reputation among the young musicians. After the August organ and brass concert, Christopher Meadows, a member of both St. John's Lutheran Church and the Bellevue High School Wind Ensemble (trumpet), asked me, the curator of the organ and the Saturday service organist, if he could start to practice on the organ. I immediately approved his request and informed the church council of the action taken. After graduation from high school, Meadows would attend Ohio Wesleyan University in Delaware, Ohio as a music education major with an emphasis on organ. After graduation from Ohio Wesleyan Meadows landed a job teaching music in the Ravenna, Ohio school district. After four years at Ravenna, he would return to his hometown and become the Bellevue High School Director of Bands. Meadow's return to Bellevue also meant bringing his considerable talent as an organist back to St. John's Lutheran Church.

With the positive response to the organ and brass choir pre-Christmas service in 2002 and with the 2003 Christmas season approaching, it was decided to plan a service for Saturday night, December 20, 2003, using the now expanded rank of young organists and a brass choir.

Although the Fourth Weekend in Advent, the service would be an early Christmas celebration, but with a *very* special talent that the 2002 service lacked, Mr. Taylor Stayton.

Taylor Stayton came to St. John's Lutheran in a rather round-about way. A native of Sydney, Ohio he started his freshman year at The Ohio State University (OSU), where he would ultimately earn his Bachelor of Music degree. During that first year at OSU he roomed with Erik Knight, whom as it has been previously noted played many times at St. John's. On one of my many trips to OSU, Knight introduced me to Stayton. Aside from being exceptionally personable, he harbored an immense talent of which I was unaware until Knight stated, "Paul, Taylor has a hell of a voice!" That was an enormous understatement! Erik asked if he could join us in our musical endeavors with the organ and I emphatically answered in the affirmative. Stayton would perform twice at St. John's Lutheran. First with the Saturday, December 20, 2003, pre-Christmas service and then at the second *Fireworks for Organ and Brass Concert* in August 2004.

After his graduation from OSU, Taylor Stayton would go on to have tremendous success in the world of opera. Here are just a few of his accolades: *Opera Today*, July, 2014…"deserving to be numbered in the short list of Rossini all-stars;" *Opera News*, October, 2011…"the very talented Taylor Stayton laser-bright timbre…" and again in July 2014, "sunny, stratospheric tenor;" finally the November, 2015 *Washington Post* commented, "A highlight was Taylor Stayton, whose bright, firm tenor rang out in one big aria of Idreno." Stayton has performed in many national and international opera venues, including *The New York Metropolitan Opera*. St. John's Lutheran Church and the Bellevue community were blessed to have a budding talent of Taylor Stayton's caliber perform and celebrate the Christmas season with us.

Once again, Wayne McCoy would be directing the brass choir and the young organists, this time with the addition of Christopher Meadows at the console. The service bulletin summed it up, "We wish to thank the musicians from St. John's, Bellevue High School, and The Ohio State University for sharing their many talents with us today."

Featured Soloist:	Taylor Stayton	
Organists:	Quenton Smith, Erik Knight, Christopher Meadows, Paul Lieber	
Brass Choir:	Wayne A. McCoy (director)	
	David Strayer, Mike Snyder, Erin Bowns, Nick Linkenhoker Rachel Smith, Renee Valko, Diana Hackenburg, David Wallingford, Brian Hopkins, Ryan Mygrant, Brent Cummins, Dan Pifer.	

Prelude:	Paul Lieber, Organ	
Opening Hymn:	Organ & Brass	"O Come All Ye Faithful"
Special Music:	Organ & Brass only	"Angels We Have Heard on High"
Hymn:	Organ	"Light One Candle to Watch for Messiah"
Hymn:	Organ & Brass	"Hark the Herald Angels Sing"
Offering Solo:		"Oh, Holy Night"
(Taylor Stayton, soloist)	Erik Knight, Organ	
Prayer:		"The Lord's Prayer", Albert Hay Malotte
(Taylor Stayton, soloist)	Erik Knight, Organ	
Communion Song:		"It Came Upon the Midnight Clear"
(Saxophonist, Jacob Knight)		
Hymn:	Organ & Brass	"Joy to the World"

The service jump-started the Christmas celebration for the parishioners and community members in attendance. At the end of the service the musicians received a standing ovation. The organists and the brass choir all did exceptionally well, but the "star of the show" for the service was Taylor Stayton! As my wife Karen put it, "His voice is angelic. It brought tears to my eyes!" As the years passed there would be thousands of opera goers stating the same thing and more about Taylor Stayton.

During the winter and early spring of 2004 St. John's Lutheran Church hosted two special concerts. On Sunday, February 29, 2004, St. John's hosted the Bellevue High School Sacred Choral Concert where The Woman's Chorus and The Concert Choir would perform under the direction of Ms. Carrie J. Sanchez. This afforded our young organists another venue to display their skills on the organ. I played the organ prelude and postlude. Two hymns would be sung by the choirs and audience during the program: *Onward Christian Soldiers*, Quenton Smith, organist and David Wallingford, pianist and *Shall We Gather at the River*, Christopher Meadows, organist, and David Wallingford, pianist.

The second concert, held on March 28, 2004, a benefit for the "Pass It on Clothing Closet", included many musicians, several church choirs and folk groups, Bellevue High School choirs, St. John's Bell Choir, a flute choir, pianists, vocal soloists, and organists put almost all of Bellevue's musical talent on display. The organ's part in this benefit program would be performed by Marlene Buck, Erik Knight, and myself:

Marlene Buck	*"Toccata on Amazing Grace"*	by Pardini
Paul Lieber	*"American Medley"*	arr. Lieber
Erik Knight	*"Grand March" from Aida*	Verdi

This concert was so successful and well attended that a second one would be planned for 2005 to again promote this worthy cause.

The spring of 2004 saw another young man brought onto the organ. David Wallingford, a tuba player in Bellevue High School's marching band and wind ensemble and a pianist in his own right, asked if he too could start to play the organ. His request was approved immediately. After graduation from Bellevue, David attended Wittenberg University where he would receive formal organ lessons. Today David Wallingford is a federal park policeman, but every time he returns to Bellevue, he runs up to the organ at St. John's and plays for a couple of hours.

From left to right Erik Knight, Quenton Smith, Chris Meadows, and David Wallingford in the Solo division of the organ. These four organists would play the Fireworks for Organ and Brass II Concert with brass choir, Taylor Stayton, soloist and Josie Widman of the Pittsburgh Symphony, playing the piccolo for Stars and Stripes Forever by Sousa. (Photo by author)

Early spring found the four young organists preparing for their next concert, *Fireworks for Organ and Brass II* scheduled for August 15, 2004. The August concert would be the young organist's most ambitious endeavor to date. It would also be the pinnacle of youth usage of St. John's organ.

The gifted Taylor Stayton, soloist, would again make an appearance and demonstrate his breadth of range in song while being accompanied by his Ohio State University roommate, Erik Knight.

A second gifted guest would also grace the August concert with her impressive talent. Josephine Marie Widman, one of the finest musicians to graduate from Bellevue High School, is the only Bellevue High School musician to earn first chair honors (flute and piccolo) in state band. Widman graduated first in the Class of 2000 at BHS. She completed her degree in music performance from Wheaton College, graduating *summa cum laude*. Following this concert Widman would pursue a master's degree from Duquesne University. Widman graciously consented to play the piccolo part to John Philip Sousa's *Stars and Stripes Forever*. Josie is the daughter of Charles Widman and Rose Mary Bauman.

The two longest tenured young organists at St. John's were Quenton Patrick Smith and Erik Louis Knight.

Quenton Smith excelled in both academics and athletics at Bellevue High School, while at the same time showing a distinct flare for keyboard instruments. Graduating seventh in the Class of 2004, he had a distinguished career as a varsity wrestler. He qualified his sophomore and senior year at BHS for the state wrestling tournament held in Columbus and had been crowned the Northern Ohio League champion in his weight class twice. Smith was also active in student government. Although he had no formal keyboard training until he started organ, he has played parts of twenty-one services and concerts at St. John's. Smith is the youngest individual at 13 ever to play the organ for a church service at St. John's.

Erik Knight displayed great musical talent all his life. He had six years of piano training early on, which aided him a great deal when he jumped to the organ. His grandfather, Louis C. Burkett, was organist at St Joseph's Roman Catholic Church in Fremont, Ohio more than thirty years. His senior year at BHS, he was first chair trumpet in the wind ensemble. Like his musical talents, he had wide ranging interests, attaining Eagle Scout status and serving as a delegate to Buckeye Boys State. Knight graduated first in the BHS Class of 2003.

The program for the August concert was a great deal more challenging than in the past. As with the previous concerts at St. John's, there would be audience participation in the form of familiar and-heart-felt songs with a patriotic bent and a brass choir. The brass choir members were:

Trumpet	French Horn	Trombone	Tuba
Christa Schultz	Amy Bowers	Ben Wallingford	David Strayer
Mike Snyder	Diana Hackenburg	Candice Wolfe	Kim Knight
Nick Linkenhoker		Robert Grasley	
Erin Bowns	**Percussion**		
Rachel Smith	Dan Pifer		
	Dane McCoy		

The concert master of ceremonies was Joseph William Smith, brother of Quenton Smith, who had now narrated his third concert at St. John's (the previous two being the *2003 Organ/Wind Ensemble Concert* and the first *Fireworks for Organ and Brass Concert* in August of 2003).

Fireworks for Organ and Brass II
Erik Knight, Quenton Smith, Christopher Meadows, and David Wallingford, organists
Introducing Taylor Stayton, Soloist
With Special Guest, Josie Widman, Piccolo
And Brass Choir Under the Direction of
Mr. Wayne A. McCoy, Director of Bands Bellevue High School

The National Anthem, verse 1 & 4   Francis Scott Key
(Quenton Smith, Organ & Brass Choir)
Fanfare For the Common Man   Aaron Copland

(Quenton Smith, Organ & Dan Pifer Timpani and Dane McCoy, Gong)

Song: Onward Christian Soldiers   Arthur S. Sullivan
(Quenton Smith, Organ & Brass Choir)
Toccata in D Minor (BWV 565)   Johann Sebastian Bach
(Quenton Smith, Organ)
*Smith received a standing ovation for his performance of this piece.
Song: America the Beautiful   Samuel A. Ward
(David Wallingford, Organ & Brass Choir)   Katherine Lee Bates
Festival Fanfare and Prelude on God of Our Fathers   J. Wayne Kerr
(Christopher Meadows, Organ)

Solo: Tenting on the Old Camp Ground   Walter Ketteredge
(Taylor Stayton, soloist & Christopher Meadows, Organ)
Song: The Battle Hymn of the Republic   Julia Ward Howe
(Christopher Meadows, Organ & Brass Choir)

INTERMISSION (10 minutes)

Prelude in Classic Style   Gordon   Ellsworth
Young (Erik Knight, Organ)
Solo: You're a Grand Old Flag   George M. Cohan
(Taylor Stayton, soloist & Erik Knight, Organ)
Toccata, from the Fifth Organ Symphony   Charles Marie Widor
(Erik Knight, Organ)
Song: Eternal Father Strong to Save   John Bacchus Dykes
(Erik Knight, Organ & Brass Choir)   William Whiting

Solo: How Great Thou Art   Carl G. Boberg
(Taylor Stayton, soloist & Erik Knight, Organ)
Stars and Stripes Forever   John Philip Sousa
(Erik Knight, Organ & Josie Widman, Piccolo)   arr. E. Power Biggs

The organists, musicians, and special guests all received a rousing standing ovation from the packed house. More than 500 people attended this, the last of the young people's organ concerts (Fire Works for Organ and Brass II) at St. John's Lutheran Church. With Erik Knight, Quenton Smith, and David Wallingford now all working on their undergraduate degrees plus working summer jobs, they didn't have the time necessary to do the needed practicing for such concerts. Christopher Meadows would continue practicing and playing occasionally at St. John's church services, particularly on Saturday nights, until he too would graduate from Bellevue High School and leave to complete his undergraduate studies at Ohio Wesleyan University. During Meadows' time at Ohio Wesleyan, he undertook extensive course work in organ.

April 17, 2005, a special event hosted by St. John's made use of the organ. The "Second Annual Benefit Concert for the Pass It on Clothing Closet" featured several different musical groups from the Bellevue High School Jazz Band, St. John's Choir, Immaculate Conception Catholic Church Folk Group, vocal solos, piano duets, and the organ. Christopher Meadows played "Festival Fanfare and Prelude on God of Our Fathers" and I played "Easter Fanfare".

Silent Film Era:

During the period running from spring 2005 to winter of 2010, St. John's did not undertake any special events which highlighted the organ. It was not until the late summer and early fall of 2009 that discussions were held about the possibility of Clark Wilson playing a silent film at St. John's during Lent. To the knowledge of the leadership of St. John's, a silent film had never been attempted at the church and, to the best of their knowledge not at any area church. After a brief discussion by the Congregational Council, it was decided that St. John's would host a silent film featuring Clark Wilson on Palm Sunday, March 28, 2010, at 7:00 p.m. which would be free and open to the public. As an aside, this silent film event was the first time that popcorn, candy, and soda pop were allowed in the Sanctuary. The Ladies of the Church made a point of telling me to remind the audience to be *very* careful, which I certainly did!

The feature film was *The King of Kings* (1927). Directed by one of Hollywood's greatest directors, Cecil B. DeMille, this superb biblical epic depicted the events leading up to Christ's crucifixion and resurrection. For 112 minutes the audience would be stepping back 83 years into Hollywood history. H.B. Warner would portray Christ in this film and DeMille would use him again in his 1956 movie, *The Ten Commandments*, as Amminadab.

At the console would be the most renowned theater organist of his time, J. Clark Wilson. At his eighteenth year as resident organist and conservator at the famed Ohio Theater in Columbus, Ohio, Wilson had also done silent film accompaniment at the Chautauqua Institution in New York, the Packard Foundation's Stanford Theater, UCLA, and the Fox Theater for the Atlanta premier of the restored silent film *Metropolis* (1927). He played *The Phantom of the Opera* (1925) in the inaugural organ concert series at LA's Walt Disney Concert Hall and has been invited back to play every year since. Wilson taught film scoring and playing at Indiana University and the University of Oklahoma.

Many hands made this special film event a huge success. Mr. Mark Woodard, President of Woodard Photographic, generously provided a large screen for this event. Other groups and individuals that contributed time, funding, and other items were St. John's Lutheran Church Congregational Council, The Reverend Karen Kaye, Paul & Karen Lieber, Charlotte Zimmerman, Dennis & Joyce Bauer, Rick & Aleta Sieger, Jan & Lois TerVeen, Ted & Marlene Buck, Sam & Bev DeBlase, Jan LaBonte, Steve & Linda Goff, Don & Josh Reiderman, Stewart & Diane Mattlage, Ralph Burns, Mike Berger, Scott Waterfield, Dale Wilson, and Charlie Corbett of Woodard Photographic.

By showcasing the organ with the inimitable Clark Wilson at the console, St. John's Lutheran provided the Bellevue community with a truly cultural, historical, and religious event that ushered in Holy Week. The evening's adventure into motion picture history started promptly at 7:00 p.m. with Wilson providing background into DeMille's making of his epic film. The lights dimmed, the credits rolled, and the organ brought the film to life. Through all one hundred and twelve minutes of the film, Wilson's command of the organ was breathtaking. From events leading up to Christ's triumphant entry into Jerusalem on what became known as Palm Sunday, the depths of his trial and crucifixion, and his glorious resurrection, Wilson elicited a kaleidoscope of voices, timbres, and colors from the 53-rank organ that dazzled the audience 150. At the conclusion of the film, Wilson received a thunderous standing ovation from the audience.

Once again, as Wilson has done every-time he has played at St. John's, he took the young organists and young musicians back up to the organ and fielded their questions, explained how he played the film, and invited them to sit down and play, so he could help them improve their skills on the organ. On March 30, 2010, I received an email from Clark Wilson expressing his thanks and how much he enjoyed the successful "organ weekend" at St. John's. He then went on to write, "I wanted to tell you, too, that it's beyond astounding that you have single-handedly caught and held the interest of so many young people for the pipe organ. Something needs to be written up about this because I think you're leading the pack, and we all ought to take some lessons from you to promote the organ RIGHT (Wilson's capitalization). You obviously "have it" where most nobody else does."

With the rousing success of the 2010 silent film *The King of Kings*, St. John's embarked on a three- year spree of hosting silent films with Clark Wilson at the console. Sticking with the Lenten season and a religious theme, it was decided to show the MGM 1925 classic, *Ben Hur*, starring Ramon Novarro as *Ben Hur* and Francis X. Bushman as the villainous Roman, Messala. In its time, *Ben Hur* proved to be a smashing world-wide success and it would be no less at St. John's in 2011.

Word had spread in the Bellevue community reflecting the success of *The King of Kings* and the attendance at *Ben Hur* would reflect that. On Sunday, March 27, 2011, the audience numbered 206 individuals for a 30% increase from the previous year. Clark Wilson did not disappoint with his accompaniment of *Ben Hur*. The organ thundered during the sea battle scenes, the chariot race (in which one of the stuntmen was killed during the filming of that scene), and Christ's Resurrection.

An editorial in the April 19, 2011, *The Bellevue Gazette* spoke to the audience reaction to *Ben Hur* and Wilson's performance:

"To the Editor: On March 27, at the St. John's Lutheran Church, a showing of the classic silent movie "Ben Hur" was shown with accomplished theater organist Clark Wilson playing the 3,500 pipe organ. What an excellent presentation.
The reason for this letter is to thank those individuals and groups for sponsoring this excellent program. I won't give names, you know who you are, but from all in attendance, we thank you so much for a wonderful evening." Shirley Lindsey, Goodrich Rd., Bellevue

Having shown two films with strong religious themes, St. John's decided to strike out in another direction. The 1925 Universal Pictures production of *The Phantom of the Opera,* starring the great Lon Chaney, Sr. as the Phantom that haunts the Paris Opera House, was shown on Sunday, March 18, 2012. At the console, Clark Wilson entertained the 186 people in the Sanctuary throughout this 1920s thriller with his usual ability to marshal every voice and color that the organ possessed.

The final entry into St. John's silent film series was the Paramount-Artcraft Picture, the 1920 horror epic *Dr. Jekyll and Mr. Hyde*, starring John Barrymore. With the showing taking place on Sunday, October 6, 2013, the film fit right into the upcoming Halloween season. John Barrymore's portrayal of Dr. Jekyll and Mr. Hyde in 1920 scared the daylights out of its audiences. Clark Wilson duly tailored his organ accompaniment to do just that, reflecting the disastrous evolution of Dr. Jekyll into the evil Mr. Hyde. The 190 people in the audience were entranced in the rollercoaster of good to evil musical themes Wilson used throughout the film. Wilson received a standing ovation at the end of the film.

In an October 16, 2013, letter sent to me by Mrs. Laura M. Stellhorn, a talented and long-serving organist at Zion Lutheran Church in Sandusky, Ohio, wrote, "The organ music with the silent movies you have arranged has been WONDERFUL (Stellhorn's capitalization) and I extend my personal thanks. It is indeed appreciated." At the end of the film, Stellhorn and several organists from the area met Wilson and expressed their pleasure and deep admiration for his abilities.

For a small mostly blue-collar/agricultural community in north central Ohio, the silent film series was a resounding success. This success in large measure reflects the exceptional talent Clark Wilson possesses and his unerring ability to pull every bit of tonal color from the 53-rank organ at St. John's Lutheran, Bellevue. Also, of great import was the foresight of the Congregational Council, the clergy, and especially those members, friends of the congregation, and businesses that helped in innumerable ways behind the scenes to make the film series a success.

The Tallar-Wilson Tonal Redesign (2018-2021)

During the period 2014-2017 the organ served the parish as originally intended for church services, weddings, and funerals. At this point in time the organ was showing signs of needing attention both mechanically and tonally.

The Bunn Minnick Pipe Organ Company of Columbus, Ohio, who had the responsibility for addressing the mechanical and tonal challenges facing the organ, only responded in part. The need to re-leather Swell, Choir, Solo, and some offset reservoirs due to "bad leather" in the late 1990s was properly completed. The tonal issues remained a stumbling block and would not be resolved until after The Bunn Minnick Pipe Organ Company closed its doors on December 31, 2017.

With their demise, St. John's looked to contract another organ provider to maintain the instrument mechanically and to address the tonal issues that had been refused. I contacted Clark Wilson and he recommended Glenn Tallar of GT Organ Associates LLC of Frankfort, Illinois. Upon my recommendation, the Congregational Council approved a two-year contract with GT Organ Associates LLC for maintenance and tuning the organ.

Pictured is the Great Division 8' Aeolian-Skinner Diapason, scale 43, rank. This set replaced a smaller Scaled 8' Prinzipal. (Photo by author)

Tonal and mechanical work on the organ commenced January 6-8, 2018, with Glenn Tallar, Clark Wilson, and me working well into the early morning hours. First came chiff removal, tonal re-voicing and finishing of the Great Principal Chorus, 4 ranks: 8' Principal – 4' Oktav – 2 2/3' Quinte – 2' Klein Oktav. This much needed work had been intended for two years. The improvement of speech in the Sanctuary with the removal of the chiff in the Great Principal Chorus was striking! Swapping of the Swell 8' Diapason (Möller rank from 1962 Bulley installation but renamed Montre) with the Pedal EM Skinner 8' (Swell) Open Diapason gave better balance and needed tonal fundamental. With the Skinner 8' Open Diapason moved to the Swell, this now utilized one of the best ranks in the organ in its proper and original role. The Swap of a large-scale Tibia with a small-scale open Flute in the Solo afforded better balance and versatility. Re-tuning all the celeste ranks to be correctly sharp in pitch, further improved ensemble sounds.

Also, a quick trip to the now closed Bunn Minnick Pipe Organ Company netted three very useful ranks: An 8' string diapason of the proper scale to replace the smaller scale Choir Diapason, a partial rank of 8' Diapason pipes of the correct scale to fill out the Pedal Diapason, and a "new" 4' Principal rank of superior tonal quality to replace the Swell 4' Prestant rank.

Much work still needed to be accomplished so from March 19-23 Tallar, Wilson, and I were back at it. At the start, our attention turned to the Choir division of the organ. Three ranks in the Choir division were to be changed out: 8' Geigen Principal, 8' Trumpet, and the 1 3/5' Tierce.

When the organ was expanded and re-leathered in 1997-98, the Choir division was left without a complete Principal Chorus and retained an 8' reed called a trumpet, but which in reality was an old and dull 8' Cornopean of 5 1/2" scale. We made the following changes to correct the Choir's tonal inadequacies: The Möller 8' Geigen Principal in the Choir was a scale 50, too small to effectively support the division. In January we had acquired a Gottfried 8' Geigen Principal, scale 45 from Bunn Minnick. Replacing the smaller scale Geigen with the larger scale rank improved presence and the stop's overall effectiveness in the organ ensemble. The 1 3/5 Tierce had been of little value, so it was replaced with a 2' Fifteenth, thus a full Principal Chorus now existed in the Choir.

The Choir lacked a true 8' Trumpet voice. The old Cornopean was just too "fat" sounding to accomplish the needed trumpet intonation. I approached the Congregational Executive Committee with a plan to facilitate the replacement of the 8' Cornopean with a real 8' Trumpet, and at the same time, honor our senior organist, Marlene Buck, on her upcoming 60th Anniversary as St. John's organist. I proposed that members of the congregation "quietly" contribute the needed funds to purchase and install the Trumpet to honor Mrs. Buck's service as organist at St. John's. The Executive Committee accepted the proposal, congregational members donated the needed funds, and the parish turned to Clark Wilson to find a Trumpet of the appropriate scale and voice. Wilson found a newer and brighter set of 4" scale, which was duly installed, voiced, and regulated. This "new" Trumpet rank added needed "fire."

The II Zymbel, located in the exposed Great Division, had rarely been used over the preceding 20 years. The principal reason for this lack of use could be attributed to rough voicing and excessive volume; it had been useless since the 1997-98 expansion of the instrument. To correct this tonal error and allow for wider use of the stop, Wilson and Tallar put in a great deal of time seamlessly melding the Great III Mixture with the now re-voiced II Zymbel (composed as a Sharp Mixture), in essence creating a five rank Mixture in the Great when the organist utilized both stops at the same time.

Work commenced on the Swell IV Plein Jeu pitched at 1'. During the 1997-98 expansion of the organ, I desired a 2' Mixture in this division for numerous valid, historic, and tonal reasons. The suggestion was not followed, and the resulting Mixture remained difficult to use and blend with the rest of the division. Beginning in March of 2018, Wilson and Tallar extended and recomposed this stop to 2' pitch, the work which would not be completed until December 2018 with the purchase of an additional rank by me to fill in the bottom octave. The entire IV Mixture was re-voiced, regulated, and tuned. For further details of the previous Mixture composition and the re-composition, see page 102.

In the Solo division two ranks were "swapped" for much improved tonal quality. Wilson and Tallar rescaled the low octave of the 2' Tibia extending the rank to a 4' pitch. A 4' Wurlitzer Concert Flute, erroneously called 4' Zauberflöte, was rescaled to become the 2' Piccolo. The results were impressive.

Marlene Buck's 60ᵗʰ Anniversary Celebration:

2018 marked the sixtieth year of Marlene Buck's service as organist at St. John's Lutheran Church. Originally the plan had been to have the festivities marking her 60 years of service at St. John's in May, but with the declining health of her husband, Ted, and his eventual passing, the anniversary celebration was postponed until Reformation Sunday October 28, 2018.

As previously noted, a "new" Choir 8' Trumpet had been purchased, installed, and used since Spring 2018. Mrs. Buck was unaware it had been purchased to honor her 60 years of service to St. John's until the October 28ᵗʰ celebratory service. Because of the generosity of many congregational members, enough funds were donated that we were also able to acquire and have installed a Pels 8' metal Rohrflute rank in the Great division of the organ in her honor. Up to this point, all the flutes in the organ at 8' pitch were constructed of wood. The removal of the Great 8' Holtz Gedeckt (an old 8' Stopped Diapason) and the installation of the metal 8' Rohrflute filled an important tonal gap in the specification.

Reformation Sunday Service and a Celebration of Marlene Buck's Sixty Years as Organist 1958-2018

Prelude: Ein Feste Burg	
Opening Hymn: A Mighty Fortress is Our God	Luther
(Christopher Meadows accompanied on Trumpet)	
Choir Anthem: Let Music Fill This Place	Martin
Service of Thanksgiving and Blessing for Marlene Buck	Pastor Mark Bogan
Sermon: "Here I Stand"	Pastor Mark Bogan
Hymn of the Day: The Church Is One Foundation	Wesley
Communion Hymn: Lord, Keep Us Steadfast in Your Word	Klug
Closing Hymn: When in Our Music God Is Glorified	Stanford

At the conclusion of the worship service, Mrs. Buck played several pieces she had a fondness for: Fantasia on *Amazing Grace*; Prelude on *"Crown Him with Many Crowns"*; *Hornpipe Humoresque: A Nautical Extravaganza for Organ*, by Noel Rawsthorne; and *God Bless America*, a perennial favorite of the Congregation (Christopher Meadows accompanied on trumpet).

With the service and Mrs. Buck's short organ recital concluded, the congregation and invited guests adjourned to the fellowship hall for a catered luncheon to cap off the day's anniversary celebration. As a final tribute, a bronze plaque affixed to the organ console read, *"In recognition of Marlene Buck's sixty years of faithful service as organist, 1958-2018."*

In those sixty years and up until her death on March 13, 2020, as both an assistant and senior organist at St. John's, Marlene played church services, weddings, funerals, and choir rehearsals numbering 8,627 and as previously noted she played several special concerts held at the church. As impressive as these numbers are her legacy contribution to St. John's and the organ world in general remains the five individuals she influenced to become organists in their own right: Elise Herrmann, Frank Stoldt, Christopher Meadows, David Wallingford, and the author.

Tonal Redesign Continues 2019-2021:

During the late summer 2019 through the good offices of Clark Wilson, I acquired three truly rare and special ranks: An Aeolian-Skinner 8' Diapason/Principal (Opus 991) and two E.M. Skinner & Son ranks, an 8' Erzähler and 8' Erzähler Celeste (Opus 550) and donate them to St. John's.

The Aeolian-Skinner 8' Diapason/Principal, originally from the four manual, 66-rank, 1939 installation at the Broadway Tabernacle, New York City, would serve as the tonal anchor for our exposed Great division. The 8' Diapason that Bunn Minnick had installed during the 1998 expansion, lacked a pure fundamental Principal tone (you could hear a flute tone in it) and was a bit too small in scale (scale 45). The scale 43 Aeolian-Skinner rank fit and supported the ensemble like a glove. Since these pipes would be exposed, the rank was taken to the Oyster Pipe Works, Ltd. of Louisville, Ohio, for minor repairs, cleaning, and painting.

The now repaired mitered sections of the 32' Contra Posaune at the Oyster Works Shop. (Photo by author)

In late July 2019, Fred Oyster and his son Nate repaired low C and low C# of the half-length 32' Contra Posaune. The mitered sections of these two pipes had collapsed on themselves, so the Oysters took apart, made new copper stems, painted them, straightened the resonator bell sections, and reassembled the two pipes at a very reasonable price. When the Aeolian-Skinner 8' Diapason/Principal needed some exterior "sprucing up" it only made good sense to again call upon the Oyster's for their expertise.

It is interesting to note that before the final repairs of the two Posaune pipes, the 32's made several stops. Originally, Bunn Minnick had transported them back to their facilities in Columbus for examination. They sent back a report to me on the collapse of the mitered sectionss due to poor zinc, and an estimate for their repair. Bunn Minnick's estimate was for several thousand dollars, which we felt was excessive. Later, the pipes were taken to The Schantz Organ Company, who gave a reasonable estimate, but were unable to take on repairs because of their previous workload. Once again, retrieving the two pipes, I took them to Fred Oyster's shop where, as previously noted, the Oysters repaired them in a couple of weeks for a reasonable charge.

From December 2-4, 2019, Tallar & Wilson installed the three "new" ranks in the organ. Rack boards were re-drilled, and the ranks were voiced, regulated, and tuned. To accommodate the two

Erzähler ranks in the Choir, the old Möller 8' Dulciana and 8' Unda Maris were removed and placed in storage. After the Erzähler installation was completed a full tuning of the entire organ readied the instrument for Christmas.

On December 6, 2019, I received the following texts from Clark Wilson. They are worth noting. "Just rolling the work over in my mind, and I'm VERY [Wilson's capitalization] happy with where we're at. The organ is sounding absolutely superb --- the ensemble sounds out now as one voice, which is just about as good as it gets. The new ranks are worthy of every bit of the work!" Wilson continued, "…I thought the organ always had a lot of built-in potential. It had

Two of the "new" ranks in the Choir division: The 8' Geigen Principal is to the right and left of the 8' Erzähler Celeste.

simply never been brought out or finely regulated. As we saw, some of the pipe choices were poor and, all in all, we have replaced and/or worked over about half the ranks at this point. The previous ideas of ensemble and blend were not good. Or they just didn't know how to get a satisfactory result. Some of the scales, both extremely large or small, were doomed to failure through natural tonal laws. It seems they thought they could use *anything* and make it work, but companies like A/S [Aeolian-Skinner & The Skinner Organ Company] didn't get where they were by doing that. I'm tickled to death that we've been able to find just what we needed so far. I am most anxious to see what a talent like Richard (Hills) will do with it."

Upon the recommendation of Wilson and Tallar, I contacted world renowned professional organist, Richard Hills of London, The United Kingdom to see if there was interest on Hills' part to play a concert at St. John's in celebration of the tonal redesign of the organ. After some emailing back and forth between myself, representing St. John's Lutheran Church, and Hills, he agreed to play a concert on Sunday afternoon, May 17, 2020. But fate, in the form of the Covid Virus worldwide pandemic, intervened forcing cancellation of the much-anticipated event.

During the December 2019 installation of the Aeolian-Skinner 8' Open Diapason on the Great, Wilson and Tallar thought it would be a real improvement to the Solo division, the string ensemble, and the organ as a whole, to acquire a large-scale matching set of 8' Gambas. During the discussions, it was remarked that it might be difficult to find these at a reasonable price.

On Saturday afternoon, February 22, 2020, and as the Covid Virus pandemic was picking up steam, I received a series of rapid-fire text from messages Wilson. "I've found you Möller 10" Solo Gambas…they are spectacular!!! Get your $$$ out…they are in New England…and what a sound…These sound just like EMS Solo Gambas or Cellos. Actually, maybe even better…they have a big rich Cello sound." Continuing, Wilson still thrilled with his find, "Sorry to be so wound up. Never thought we would ever find these…get out the rack board drills!"

The Möller 8' Grosse Gamba (73 pipes) and 8' Gamba Celeste (61 pipes), were purchased from Mr. Norman Shanklin. These two ranks were from MP Möller Opus 5830 (1930) from Old

South (now First) Congregational Church in Worcester, Massachusetts. Pictured is C of the 8' Gross Gamba with the name "Whittington Oct-10-1930" scrawled on it. Opus 5830 details were as follows: Electro-pneumatic chests, four manuals, six divisions (Great, Swell, Choir, Solo, Echo, & Pedal), 46 total ranks, and 3223 pipes, OHS Organ ID-32101. We hoped to possess the ranks by the first week of April and to have them installed before the Hills Concert on May 17. But with the Covid-19 pandemic taking hold in much of the United States, including Ohio and New Hampshire, the time frame changed drastically. Finally, the nation started to gradually open-up, Norm Shanklin graciously brought the two ranks from New Hampshire to Chardon, Ohio, where St. John's took possession of the Gambas on Thursday, June 11, 2020.

To incorporate the two Gambas into the Solo division of the organ, we removed two rescaled, unused, made-up ranks, a 2 2/3' Nazard and a 1 3/5' Tierce. Oyster Pipe Works, Ltd. replaced the tuning collars on the bottom octave of both ranks plus rounding out a couple of pipes from each rank.

Wilson, Tallar, Jaret Schroeder, and I worked for two and a half days during the third week of July completing the following work: installation of the 8' Grosse Gambas; removal of dents and fitted tuning collars; main Solo chest pressure raised from 6 ½" to 8"; initial regulation on other Solo ranks; tested "new" Möller 4' Octave in the Great; cone-tuned Swell 4' Principal and Mixture pipes cut to length and fitted with slide tuners.

The "new" Möller 4' Octave, Opus 8100 (1950), built for the First Presbyterian Church of Jeanette, PA comprised of 12 ranks, 883 pipes, 2 manuals, and 3 divisions, OHS Organ ID-34930, was tested in the Great and brought the needed color lacking in the existing 4' Octave. Through the good offices of Fred Oyster, the author and his wife Karen purchased this rank and donated it to St. John's in honor of their son LTC Michael Hosang (ret.) and his wife Jessica. Oyster's cleaned the pipes and made new stainless-steel tuning collars for the entire rank. Tallar and Wilson installed, regulated, and tuned the 4' Octave rank on September 8, 2020. Its inclusion in the Great Principal Chorus added much needed presence and color. With this final rank replacement, the Great Principal Chorus can only be described as stellar.

At this time, the tonal finishing of the fluework in the Solo division was completed, the wind pressure raised on the main Solo chest, and low A of the 8' Gamba Celeste installed.

Conclusion

"It is relatively simple to provide colorful stops but not at all simple to blend them into an artistic and cohesive whole."

— G. Donald Harrison, Aeolian-Skinner Company

As a parish, St. John's Lutheran Church has been blessed with congregants who have always desired and supported the use of a pipe organ for worship. Using instruments of vastly different scope and configuration over the past 125 years, a group of thirteen dedicated and talented organists carried out the mission of leading the musical component of the worship service to the best of their ability and to the Glory of the Lord.

Of the four pipe organs prior to the 2018-2021 Tonal Redesign used by St. John's Lutheran Church, the only extant and fully playable organ resides in St. Peter's Lutheran Church outside of Monroeville, Ohio. It is believed to be one of the very last surviving unaltered examples of John Sole's pipe organ production. The Sole organ provided yeoman service for worship, concerts, and special celebrations from 1895-1933, including the much celebrated 50th Anniversary of the parish founding, and remains the only tracker action instrument ever to see service at St. John's. But the Bellevue parish outgrew the organ, and to be frank, St. John's donation of the Sole organ to St. Peter's Lutheran Church likely saved it from being parceled out piecemeal or, worse yet, junked, a demise so many other fine instruments of the past have suffered.

St. John's replaced the Sole Organ with the Knapp Memorial Organ in late 1933 and it served the parish until the old red brick church was torn down in 1959 to make way for a "new" church edifice. Although I was able to track the use of the Knapp Memorial Organ while it served the congregation at St. John's, finding the exact history and background of this instrument prior to its installation at St. John's along with the organ's specification has proved more than just elusive, but downright impossible, even with the expert help of William Van Pelt of the Organ Historical Society. I can state that the organ was an electro-pneumatic, two manual instrument of twelve stops.

For the newly built church Sanctuary (1962) and at the recommendation of the organ committee, Jullian Bulley of the Toledo Pipe Organ Company installed a four manual, 36-rank organ. As previously noted, this instrument was composed of pipework from several organs, largely Möller, and an excellent Möller four manual console. The pipework and the console would serve as the "core" of the Bunn Minnick expansion and renovation, and with modifications, of the 2018-2020 tonal redesign.

Although the TPOC organ served the parish well from 1962-1997, the installation left something to be desired. The entire organ rested behind a cloth/wood façade with no exposed Great. The divisions, Great, Swell, and Choir "ran into each other" having no dividing walls between them. The winding and electrical wiring ran haphazardly across the floor of the pipe chamber. Before the Great could be tuned, three large pipes of the 8' Great Diapason had to be removed from the chest to provide access to tune that division. After 30 years of use, the TPOC instrument started showing its age, plus the previously noted problems with the installation came to the fore. Bulley recommended a re-leathering of the organ at an estimated cost of $40,000 (phone conversation with Marlene Buck and later a second call with me). These events triggered the establishment of an organ committee in the mid-1990s to search for other organ companies that could inspect the instrument and provide guidance. The organ committee turned to the Schantz Organ Company, Orville, Ohio and the Bunn Minnick Pipe Organ Company, Columbus, Ohio. Eventually at the recommendation of the organ committee, St. John's chose Bunn Minnick, principally because Bunn Minnick would keep/re-cycle the bulk of the pipework, retain and expand the Möller console, and when possible, reuse the well-built Möller chests.

Bunn Minnick provided St. John's with a large and versatile instrument. On the positive side, the winding and the electrical outlay were vastly improved and still serve the organ well today. Their physical layout of the organ enhanced and facilitated easier tuning. Walls were erected between the Swell, Solo, and Choir divisions allowing for much improved volume control. Bunn Minnick expanded the Solo Division from four ranks to twelve ranks inclusive of two fine EM Skinner ranks, the 8' French Horn and the 8' English Horn. Utilizing two local companies, Thomas Steel and Zimmerman Construction, they constructed an exposed Great which provided greater versatility of use, enhanced congregational singing, while adding an architecturally beautiful façade in which all pipes speak.

Along with the improvements made during the Bunn Minnick renovation and expansion, the non-worship use of the organ expanded dramatically: Three Bellevue High School Wind Ensemble/Organ Concerts (two played by Marlene Buck and one featuring Brett Valliant); a concert of orchestral transcriptions with Clark Wilson at the console; two summer "Young Organists Concert"; and four silent films performed by Wilson.

The principal reason for the parish turning to Bunn Minnick to renovate the organ at St. John's, was the company's ideal of recycling older pipework, a fundamentally sound philosophy. The unsuccessful attempt at blending varying scales, pressures, and types of pipework in this instrument, however, led to the eventual need for the tonal redesign of the organ during 2018-2021.

The redesign program encompassed extensive tonal finishing and replacement of inappropriate or incorrectly scaled ranks. This included both flue and reed stops, and in all divisions. The most important aspects, the Diapason choruses Great, Swell and Choir divisions, are now excellent and were completed with the replacement of the Great 4' Octave rank with the Möller Opus 8100 4' Octave. Of the 53 ranks comprising the organ, fully 29 ranks were impacted during this tonal redesign inclusive of installation, regulating and voicing of replacement ranks, and regulation and voicing of existing ranks:

> GREAT: 8' Diapason, 8' Rohrflute, 4' Octave, 2 2/3' Quinte, 2' Super Octave, and
>> total regulation changes on the III Mixture and II Sharp Mixture
>
> SWELL: 8' Diapason, 8' Bourdon, 4' Principal, and IV Mixture recomposed and
>> extended to 2'
>
> CHOIR: 8' Geigen Diapason, 8' Erzähler, 8' Erzähler Celeste, 4' Octave, 2' Fifteenth, 8' Trumpet

SOLO: 8' Grosse Gamba, 8' Gamba Celeste, 4' Tibia Flute, 2' Piccolo, and raised the wind
     pressure to 8" on main Solo chest
PEDAL: 8' Principal, Cut 1 rank from Mixture

The 2018-2021 Tonal Redesign Project brought a true ensemble out of the instrument, one commensurate with a large symphonic, possibly "American Classic" type organ. The cohesive ensemble and solo combinations speak for themselves!

As stated in an overview of the work completed from J.C. Wilson & Associates and GT Organ Associates dated July 19, 2020:

"The English, and to a lesser degree, American schools are most strongly reflected now. The recent and probably most stunning overall addition is in the Grosse Gamba ranks in the Solo, two indispensable and spectacular ranks absolutely required in an organ of this magnitude.

With their commanding sound the string ensembles now stand with the finest anywhere. We believe this organ to be among the really fine instruments of its type. While not of a single brand, it is still proof positive of what is truly worth saving and re-using. **Many of the voices are superior to anything being produced today**, and the organ should proudly serve and hold its own under any circumstances for decades to come."

The impact/influence of the four organs utilized by St. John's Lutheran from 1895 to the present, cannot be limited to, or viewed as, strictly a tool for religious services. Yes, to serve worship services remained throughout their tenure the principal *raison d'être*. But a careful examination of their past use elicits a somewhat more circumspect analysis as to their role at St. John's and the effect they have had on parishioners, youth, and community members alike, especially during and after the 1997-98 renovation and expansion.

From 1895 until the renovation and expansion of the TPOC instrument, the organs use had been limited to worship services, weddings, funerals, and church historical anniversaries. The only exceptions during that time frame being the organ dedication concert for the TPOC instrument in 1962 and the Bellevue community's 1976 Bicentennial concert held at St. John's and then the organ was used only for the finale, the community choir singing Peter J. Wilhousky's arrangement of *The Battle Hymn of the Republic*.

During and after 1997-98, use of the organ took an evolutionary and quantum leap. Removal, fund raising, and re-installation of the organ brought the congregation closer together with the shared goal of improving the musical component of the worship service. The active participation of congregational members brought to light what a monumental job removal, repair, and expansion of the organ truly was. Lutheran youth and BHS student athletes played an important part in removal and re-installation phases of the organ project. Thus, all participants took pride and ownership in this exemplary project.

Not only did worship services of all types benefit from the more versatile Bunn Minnick organ, but the community did as well. The church council made the fundamentally wise decision for a broader use of this musical asset that would eventually touch many individuals and the Bellevue community at large. The Organ/BHS Wind Ensemble Concerts of 1999, 2001, and 2003; Clark Wilson's Orchestral Transcriptions Concert; BHS students and parish youth playing part or full church services usually with brass accompaniment from BHS band members; two Summer Young Organists Concerts with brass choirs, in addition to vocal and instrumental soloists; and four silent films performed by Wilson.

The last chapter in the history of the organs of St. John's was the essential tonal re-design of the Bunn Minnick instrument by Wilson and Tallar. As previously mentioned, the Bunn Minnick instrument faced mechanical and tonal issues. The leather in the reservoirs of the Great division was failing and their re-leathering has been completed. With the 2018-2021 tonal re-design plan successfully completed, the organ's clarity of tone and sound is unparalleled, and it now speaks with one voice. In addition to the excellent tonal and technical expertise of Wilson and Tallar, pipework from some of the Twentieth Century's premier American organ builders: Aeolian-Skinner, Austin, EM Skinner, EM Skinner & Son, Gottfried, MP Möller (almost half the organ), and Wurlitzer provided these gifted technicians with superlative material with which to complete their tonal re-design. It is a fitting evolution and tribute to the organs that graced the parish of St. John's Lutheran Church and the community of Bellevue with their music.

Organ Specification, 2021

Compass: Manual, 61 notes; Pedal, 32 notes
53 ranks; 3,489 pipes

II. Great: exposed, 12 ranks – 756 pipes
 16 Violone
  8 Open Diapason, sc. 43
  8 Gemshorn
  8 Rohrflute
  8 Flute Celeste II (Choir)
  8 Erzähler Celeste II (Choir)
  4 Octave
  4 Chimney Flute
  2 2/3 Quinte
  2 Super Octave
 III Mixture (1 1/3)
 II Sharp Mixture (1/2)
 16 Contra Trumpet tc (enclosed in Choir)
  8 Trompette Héroique (Great)
  8 Trumpet (enclosed in Choir)
  8 Harmonic Tuba (Solo)*
  4 Clarion (enclosed in Choir)
   Great Unison Off
  4 Great to Great
    Non-couple

III. Swell: enclosed, 13 ranks – 937 pipes
 16 Bourdon Doux
  8 Open Diapason, sc. 45
  8 Bourdon
  8 Viol D' Gamba
  8 Viol Celeste (tc)
  4 Principal
  4 Flute Harmonique
  2 Doublette
  2 Flute A' Bec
 II Sesquialtera (derived)
 IV Mixture (2)
 16 Posaune
  8 Trompette Héroique (Great)
  8 Trompette
  8 Oboe
  8 Vox Humana
  4 Clairon
   Tremulant
 16 Swell to Swell
   Swell Unison Off
  4 Swell to Swell

I. Choir: enclosed, 12 ranks – 720 pipes
 16 Contra Erzähler
  8 Geigen Principal, sc. 45
  8 Concert Flute
  8 Flute Celeste
  8 Erzähler
  8 Erzähler Celeste (tc)
  4 Octave
  4 Flute D' Amour
  2 2/3 Nasat
  2 Fifteenth
  2 Flautino
  1 1/3 Larigot
  1 Fugara
  8 Trompette Héroique (Great)

Choir – CONT.
  8 Trumpet
  8 Clarinet
   Tremulant
   Zimbelstern
 16 Choir to Choir
   Choir Unison Off
  4 Choir to Choir

IV. Solo: enclosed, 12 ranks, 684 pipes
 16 Quintadena
  8 Stentorphone, sc. 38
  8 Flauto Mirabilis
  8 Quintadena
  8 Gross Gamba

Solo – CONT.

8 Gamba Celeste
8 Viole D' Orchestra
8 Viol Celeste
IV Grande String 8 (All Solo String Ranks)
4 Tibia Flute
2 Piccolo
16 Trombone*
16 Trompette Héroique (Great)
8 Harmonic Tuba*
8 Trompette Héroique (Great)
*On 12" of wind
**16-8-4 Trompette Héroique are non-coupling*

8 French Horn*
8 English Horn*
4 Tuba Clarion*
4 Trompette Héroique (Great)
Tremulant
Chimes
16 Solo to Solo
Solo Unison Off
4 Solo to Solo

Pedal: 4 ranks – 212 pipes

32 Contra Bass, Resultant
32 Echo Bourdon, Resultant
16 Wood Diapason
16 Subbass
16 Violone (Great)
16 Quintadena (Solo)
16 Bourdon Doux (Swell)
8 Principal
8 Major Flute
8 Bass Flute
8 Gemshorn (Great)
8 Bourdon (Swell)
5 1/3 Quinte (Swell)
4 Octave

4 Flute
2 Super Octave
III Rauschpfeife
32 Contra Posaune (Swell)
32 Grand Harmonics (derived)
16 Tuba Profunda (Solo)
16 Posaune (Swell)
8 Harmonic Tuba (Solo)
8 Trompette Héroique (Great)
8 Trompette (Swell)
4 Tuba Clarion (Solo)
4 Clairon (Swell)
4 Clarinet (Choir)

Expression: Swell, Choir, Solo, Master Expression (Solo Shoe), and Crescendo Pedal.
        Master Expression reversible piston.
Mechanicals: Solid State capture combination action with 10 levels of memory; general (18),
        divisional (6) and cancel pistons; toe studs general (10), pedal (6), and cancel.
        Great, Swell, Choir, and Solo to Pedal reversible pistons and toe studs; all Pedal
        32s have reversible pistons and toe studs; Zimbelstern, sforzando, and tutti
        reversible pistons and toe studs; general cancel and set pistons.
Couplers: Great, Swell, Choir, and Solo 8 and 4 to Pedal
        Swell, Choir, and Solo 16, 8, and 4 to Great
        Swell 16, 8, and 4 to Choir
        Great 8 and Solo 8 to Choir
        Swell 8 to Solo
        Solo 8 to Swell
Console prepared for Antiphonal Division

Pictured on the south wall of the Choir is the 16' Wood Open. The bearded pipes On the left are part of the 8' Trumpet.

From right to left are the Choir 8' Clarinet, 4' Octave, 8' Erzähler, and the 8' Flute Celeste ranks. (Photos by author)

In the Swell 32' Contra Posaune on left and 16' Posaune on right. Part of the 16' Bourdon Doux at rear and upper part of the chamber.

Left to right, Swell 8' Open Diapason, 8' Vax Humana, and 8' Oboe ranks. (Photos by author)

From back to front, Great 4' Octave, 2 2/3' Quinte, 2' Super Octave, III Mixture, and II Sharp Mixture.

From Left to right, Great 8' Trompette Heroïque, 16' Violone, 8' Gemshorn, and 8' Open Diapason. (Photos by author)

Part of Solo main chest with 16' Tuba Profunda in the background; the tall string ranks directly in front of the Tuba are the 8' Grosse Gamba and 8' Gamba Celeste.

From left to right, the Solo 8' English Horn and 8' French Horn. To the right of the French Horn is the 8' Pedal Principal. (Photos by author)

The Sole Organ at St. Peter's Lutheran Church

Above, the Sole Organ circa 1900 at St. John's Lutheran Church, Bellevue. The photo on the right is the Sole organ as it is today at St. Peter's. The 8' Diapason pipes that made up the façade at St. John's were retained by that parish. The present-day photo shows the replacement 8' Diapason pipes at St. Peter's. Although functional, they are not yet playable. (Photo courtesy of Larry Claus)

(Photo by author)

Swell Division right to left, 8' Oboe, 4' Flute Harmonique, 8' Salicional, and 8' Stopped Diapason.

(Photo by author)

Pastors of St. John's Lutheran Church (1864-2017)

Jacob Dornbirer	1864-1869	Kenneth E. Nosworthy	1970-1973
Christian Buechler	1869-1883	Roland Troike	1974-1977
Johann J. Sutter	1883-1884	Fred Zangmeister	1977-1982
Henry J. Sutter	1884-1892	Roger K. Miller	1978-1982
W.E. Schuette, DD	1893-1901	T. Rene Meyer	1980-1983
W.H. Lehmann, DD	1902-1910	U. Luther Siefkes	1983-1987
John W. Kuntz	1910-1919	Steven Schick	1983-1985
Harold W. Rose, DD	1920-1924	Marvin Miller	1986-1990
A.A. Ahn	1925-1934	David Wietelmann	1988-2002
Paul A. Rempe	1934-1949	Stuart Luce	1992-1997
Rennix L. VanScoy	1949-1952	Henry C. Seibert	2000-2004
T. Rene Meyer	1953-1965	Michael Pozzuto	2005-2007
Richard M. Billings	1963-1975	Karen A. Kaye	2008-2010
Herbert Wolber	1966-1969	Juli Lejman-Guy	2011-2017

Bunn Minnick Employees and Individuals Associated With the 1997-1998 Organ Project

Boyd Frank Akers	Roy E. Graves	Mylan J. Peterson
Robert W. Bunn, Jr.	Shawn A. Hawkins	Marcella S. Redman
A.J. Cannaday	David T. Hill	Lillian B. Reynolds
Don D. Capelle	Linda M. Hill	David B. Schneider
Karen A. Freudigman	Victor K. John	Paul E. Taynor, Jr.
Jennifer Fry	Leo J. Klise, Jr.	James Timothy Trout
Arline K. Fuhr	Brian A. Kovats	Shawn Van Curen
Katie S. Fuhr	Richard H. Locke	Craig M. Vanderveen
Scott D. Fuhr	Jack W. May	David S. Waldroop
Sean J. Gaddis	Dennis C. Nader	Thurlow B. Weed
Evan S. Gorsuch	Kenneth F. Peacock	J. Clark Wilson
Scott N. Gorsuch	Robert A. Peacock	Jessie M. Wright

*Philip D. Minnick, President, Bunn Minnick Pipe Organ Company

Wind Ensemble Musicians 1999, 2001, and 2003

1999

Flute
Josie Widman
Elizabeth Studer
Kristen Englehart
Kelly Harmon
Jessica Leckrone
Andrea Buckner

Oboe
Shaun Smith

Clarinet
Veronica Robinson
Laura Winters
Andrea Berkey
Bill King
Emily Valko
Emily Hassinger
Jennifer Robinson
Doug Smith

Alto Clarinet
Haley Steinbauer

Bass Clarinet
Adrienne Felder
Alicia Meyer
Jared Mygrant

Alto Sax
Curtis Rospert
David Riegel
Courtney Dietzel
Catherine Bibb

Tenor Sax
Philip Shumway
Kyle Fries

Bari Sax
Heather Riegel

French Horn
Danyelle Dauch
Ashley Egbert
Brandi Cooper
Brenda Ritter

Trumpet
Logan Buck
Pam Hill
Alison Manasco
Joel Wietelmann
Jennifer Allison
Becky Boger
Tim Gerhardstein
Kevin Rowe
Jen Lyons

Trombone
Julie Maike
Libby Rivera
Evan Beck
Kevin Cloud

Euphonium
Alex Beck
Steve Goff II
Tim Moyer

Tuba
Paul Custer
Phil Manning

Percussion
Amanda Felder
Julia Haar
Brian Bond
Val Gohlike
Jason Iannello
Megan Greene
Mike Mira
Brian Decker

Mallets
Sara Bond
Stacey Kudro

2001 Concert

Flute
Kristen Englehart
Andrea Buckner
Erica Sage
Laura Huff
Stephanie Shaffer
Mandy Hart

Bass Clarinet
Jessica Walters
Heather Martin

Alto Sax
Amanda Greiner
David Riegel
Curt Hill
Courtney Dietzel

Trombone
Evan Beck
David Wallingford
Andrew Bishop
Aaron Ammaniti

Euphonium
Tim Moyer

Oboe
Shaun Smith

Bassoon
Emily Hassinger

Clarinet
Veronica Robinson
Andrea Berky
Heather Waterman
Janna Greene
William King
Doug Smith
Katie Custer
Gabrielle Reamer
Emily Valko

Alto Clarinet
Erin Mathias
Karen Binsack

Tenor Sax
Elizabeth Musick
Lydia Freeze

Bari Sax
Joy Bolen

French Horn
Emily Foisy
Amy Bowers
Renee Valko

Trumpet
Joel Wietelmann
Erik Knight
Tim Gerhardstein
Logan Buck
Christa Schultz
Brandon Good

Josh Russell

Tuba
Eric Williamson
Heather Riegel

Percussion
Brian Bond
John Maike
Adam Buchanan
Eric Daniel
Cassondra Norman
Kyle Musick

Mallets
Doug Smith
Beth Hansen

2003 Concert

Flute
Laura Huff
Katy Klein
Dana Freeman
Erin Riegel
Sandra Allen
Amanda Pensiero

Bass Clarinet
Tonya Barnhart
Nikki Wheeler

Alto Clarinet
Karen Binsack

Alto Sax
Amanda Greiner*
Nancy Daniels
Jon Smith*

Oboe
Kevin Owens

Bassoon
Andrew Zilch

Trumpet
Erik Knight*
Christa Schultz*
Michael Snyder*
Erin Bowns*
Brandon Good*
Rachel Smith*

Trombone
Andrew Bishop*
Randy Yates*
Justin Fisher*
Aaron Ammanniti*

Clarinet
Joshua Jones
Heather Waterman
Amy Bowers
Renee Valko
Gabrielle Reamer
Brittani Covella
Malory Rister
Adrian Ortiz
Molly Linkenhoker
Amanda McFarland

Tuba
David Wallingford*
Ryan Mygrant

Percussion
Adam Buchanan*
Dane McCoy
Leslie King

Andrew Eisenhower
Rachel Norman
Curt Hill*

Tenor Sax
Lydia Freeze*
Robert Buckner*

Euphonium
Joshua Russell
Nick Linkenhoker
Matt Riegel
Zach Guenther

French Horn
Emily Foisy*
Diana Hackenburg

Dan Pifer*
Sarah Aigler
Grace Fry
Nolan Baum
Beth Magers

Mallets
Elizabeth Yingling

Additional Jazz Musicians
Brian Hopkins*
Kayla Newkirk*

Bari Sax
Kristofer Mygrant*

*Denotes Jazz Band Members

Swell Mixture Composition

Bunn Minnick 1997-98 IV Plein Jeu Composition at 1' Pitch

I	22	19	15	12	8	1
II	26	22	19	15	12	8
III	29	26	22	19	15	12
IV	33	29	26	22	19	15
	13	12	12	12	5	7

Wilson-Tallar Re-composition of Swell IV Mixture at 2' Pitch

	15	15	15	15
I	19	12	8	1
II	22	15	12	8
III	26	19	15	12
IV	29	22	19	15
	13	24	12	12

Ranks installed during the 2018-2021 and Citations

Great Division:

8' Open Diapason, Aeolian Skinner, Opus 991 (1939)

> Given by Paul & Karen Lieber in Honor of our granddaughters
> Isabella Rose Hosang and Evelyn Louise Hosang

8' Rohrflute, Pels

> Given by the Congregation of St. John's Lutheran Church in Honor
> of and Recognition of Marlene Buck's sixty years of dedicated service
> as parish organist purchased from Shawn Kenny

4' Octave, MP Möller, Opus 8100 (1950)

> Given by Paul & Karen Lieber in Honor of our son LTC Michael
> Hosang (ret.) and his wife Jessica Hosang

Swell Division:

4' Principal, of European manufacture and design

> Purchased by St. John's Lutheran Church in Honor of and Recognition
> of the thirteen individuals who served as parish organists from 1895-2020

2 2/3' rank for extending IV Mixture to 2'; Purchased from Shawn Kenny and
> donated by Paul & Karen Lieber

Choir Division:

8' Geigen Principal, A. Gottfried & Company

> Given by Paul & Karen Lieber in Memory of Paul's brother
> Richard "Mike" Lieber

8' Erzähler, EM Skinner & Son, Opus 550 (#267 Quincy), 1941

> Given by Paul & Karen Lieber in Memory of Paul & Ruth Lieber,
> Ralph & Eunice Lieber, Rose Lieber, Bertrum & Mable Newell,
> and Ray & Madeline Boose

8' Erzähler Celeste, EM Skinner & Son, Opus 550 (#267 Quincy), 1941

> Given by Paul & Karen Lieber in Honor of Dr. Benjamin James Wendt, MD

4' Octave, Organ Supply Industries, formerly A. Gottfried & Company

> Given by Paul Lieber in Honor of his wife Karen

8' Trumpet, Organ Supply Industries, 4" scale

> Given by the Congregation of St. John's Lutheran Church in Honor
> of and Recognition of Marlene Buck's sixty years of dedicated service
> as parish organist

Solo Division:

8' Grosse Gamba, MP Möller, Opus 5830 (1930)
> Given by Paul & Karen Lieber in memory and honor of Milton & Charlotte Zimmerman who faithfully supported the St. John's parish during their lifetimes. Of note was their enthusiastic support for the organ, including expansion, maintenance, concerts, and use by youth.

8' Gamba Celeste, MP Möller, Opus 5830 (1930)
> Given by Paul & Karen Lieber in honor of congregational members who helped Paul during the 2018-2021 Tonal Redesign: Mike Berger, Lennie Bowers, Bill Braddock, Jake Doster, Sam Doster, Zach Eskins, Gunnar Lilly, Kegan Lilly, Rich Lilly, Zarek Lilly, Christopher Meadows, Kaden Miller, Mason Miller, and Jan TerVeen

Index

The index has been constructed without a line referencing "St. John's Lutheran Church". In the author's view, with "St. John's" appearing on most of the pages, it would be redundant to list every page citing the parish.

Printed in the USA
CPSIA information can be obtained
at www.ICGtesting.com
LVHW070033291023
762414LV00008B/28